A Poacher's Way

A POACHER'S WAY

JOHN BAILEY

The Crowood Press

First published in 1995 by
The Crowood Press Ltd
Ramsbury, Marlborough
Wiltshire

British Library Cataloguing in Publication Data

A catalogue record for this book is available from
the British Library.

ISBN 1 85223 859 3

Line-drawings by Paul Groombridge.

Typeset and designed by D & N Publishing, Ramsbury, Wiltshire.

Printed by Redwood Books, Trowbridge.

Contents

1

Shino and Me

*I*n the sixties we did remarkably fine things and often remarkably stupid ones, too: the air had a licence to it then that drugged any rational senses, that led some of us from one wild escapade to the next extraordinary excess. I myself fell victim to this peculiar disease towards the end of the decade, a period that haunts me still and which this book is meant to exorcize. Truthfully, when autumn nights are dark, with rustling winds and the pattering of rain at the window, I find it hard not to leave the house, wander down the track and into the woods like I did then. Woods are my friends, and I have never been able to live away from them since that time.

This is the account of perhaps eighteen months in my life when I was a very young lad; a time when I became the accomplice of a most remarkable man in an equally extra-ordinary place. I saw and learnt things that have never left me and I still look back on those months as, in many ways, the very best ones of my entire life. The book that follows, however, does not belong to me at all, but to Shino, so much the dominating force in my life that I simply revolved around him, rather like the earth does the sun. Certainly it was from Shino that I received all my inspiration.

So, who was – or I should say, is – Shino? The putting of all these thoughts down on to paper comes from a chance meeting a few months back when permission for this book was granted. I recognized Shino immediately, even though twenty-five years had passed since we worked so intimately together. He is a man who will always be unmistakable, impossible to forget or to ignore. Six foot three or thereabouts, fourteen stone then and perhaps fifteen now, and still with the same shock of blond hair and dazzling blue eyes that hint at a Danish ancestry so common to many of the folk of this region.

Even now, just as I remembered, his face and forearms are tanned; tanned, you feel, through to the bone by a life spent constantly in the outdoors. No passing holiday colour this but something ingrained, as permanent as a nose or a pair of hands, a badge of the outdoor man. Not surprisingly it was in a pub that we met again; over the general throng I heard Shino's voice and explosion of a laugh, and was in no doubt that I was in his company again after so long. He was still surrounded by rogues and countryside villains, the type of men who have nothing in particular to do at 2.30 on a Monday afternoon but put down a beer or two, share some stories and wait for evening to draw in. Shino, though, maintains that he is pretty respectable these days, and it is true that there are not many of us now left who remember him by the nickname that was all but his exclusive title a quarter of a century ago.

A quarter of a century ago almost exactly it was that I knocked on his cottage door, looking for occupation, fresh from college. After three years of city life I had been longing to get back to the country again, and had found myself one of the most peculiarly unsatisfactory jobs I could have dreamt of. For two or three weeks I had been working in a large barn, close to the roar of the sea, supervising forty women who spent the daylight hours cleaning Brussels sprouts. It was a crazily chaotic job and the women ran me absolutely ragged with their complaints, their stories, their flirtations and their constant manipulation of a twenty-one year old who had been arrogant enough to think he knew about women. I was exhausted, desperate, and was directed to Shino by members of the village football team for which I had begun to play.

By day, Shino was a worm-digger, one of those hardy men who make a living from the flat, sandy shorelines of this county. At the time I thought it was amazing that he accepted me straight off, and I was out there the next morning as soon as the tide had withdrawn, with fork and bucket, digging like a dervish for the big, rubbery, sinuous lugworms that we would sell by the thousand to coastal long-liners. But although the hours were short, the work was cripplingly hard: if a living were to be made, then at least a thousand worms had to be dug in two, three, or at the most four hours. Soon my hands became scarred and cracked, and the salt got into the wounds so deep that at times they would be sporting twenty or thirty strips of plaster. I can look now and still see calluses and scars on my hands that even after this length of time have never healed and, to this day, my back still screams at the sight of a fork.

That was what Shino and I did by day: by night, however, it was quite a different affair and come sundown, Shino moved into his second occupation. He was a poacher, and it was made quite clear to me that if I wanted to dig with him, then I had to walk at night with him. I soon saw why he had taken me on, untried, untested: he had lost one stooge, another young lad, to the navy and he needed a regular underling to carry out many of the less intricate and demanding tasks. Often Shino liked to work alone, and frequently he went out with a regular partner, the massively bearded Mears; but there were always tasks for the willing apprentice that I soon became.

9

Now, I have a fair amount to say about poaching before we go any further, because there are some strange misconceptions. There is still a general belief that city poachers descend on country woodlands and estates in highly efficient, motorized gangs quite capable of stripping them of every wild bird within an hour or so. This extraordinary idea probably comes down in the mists of time, certainly from the last century when it is quite true that on occasion groups of starving, labouring men did band together for a lightning raid on a nearby wood. But this is all D. H. Lawrence stuff, though there were well-publicized clashes between poachers on the one hand and police and keepers on the other. These old tales have probably been given strength by the undoubted activities of some Scottish salmon poaching gangs who do operate in a highly mobilized, totally callous way, and who often receive a great deal of publicity.

For the most part, however, the presence of these urban poaching gangs in our English countryside is a myth. Today there is not the poverty and suffering that would drive men out in this way, to risk so much to feed a family. And for those above the bread-line, never think that poaching makes a man affluent, even now, especially if he has to split the proceeds with so many others. Remember, too, that the whole secret of a poacher's success is intimate knowledge of the woods he is working. The idea of complete strangers, from towns, descending into uncharted woodland in the dark and pulling off a successful operation is absolutely laughable. Within minutes the gang would be separated, confused, disorientated and headed for home ... so let's not bother with talk of gangs again.

The other image is quite different: this is of some bucolic mischief-maker who does no real harm to anybody, fumbling along with the odd trap or snare or shotgun, taking the occasional rabbit or pheasant for the pot and doing less harm, overall, than a single fox or magpie. The fact that nobody now needs to steal to make a living does little to cloud this idea of the country poacher as a character to be winked at, if not positively encouraged. Even so, there is some truth in this image, and the amateur still exists in the countryside; though a man like this will in fact poach very infrequently and perhaps take no more than a dozen birds in a whole year. He is almost certainly not a very good poacher, nor a practised one, but his unpredictability probably ensures him a lifetime of undetected success. What birds the amateur takes one might guess do little more than help him or his neighbours out at Christmas, and merely bolster his image as a derring-do sort of fellow.

Shino, however, was the type of poacher that keepers really fear. Shino was the country professional, the class of man who really takes his share from every woodland. And of all the professionals he was probably, at that time and in that place, the king. The professionals are clever and they can conduct their business for years without fear of capture. Providing there are sufficient well-stocked shooting estates around them, they can vary their attack night after night, and this element of surprise renders them almost uncatchable. The professional will work an area that he knows well, intimately even, very rarely more than ten miles or so from home. Woods will abound and he will know every single avenue, almost each twig; and the rural professional has everything in his favour.

Knowledge is all: as a lad, Shino was welcomed onto every estate as a beater, singing his little heart out to scare the birds up for the guns. But even as a ten year old he probably knew where his future would lie, and he was making mental notes as he worked. Even then his mind was fixing the position of each keeper's cottage, and the character and reputations of the keepers themselves; marking down for future reference the release pens, the best coverts, the ways of entry and the means of escape.

The fact that Shino's woods were so plentiful and close by meant that the element of surprise was always his: he need never drive to his nightly work but could cycle or even walk, leaving no clues in the lane outside the woodlands. All around he had friends in cottages who would take the game or help him out if the pace became hot. Living on the job Shino could mount lightning-quick attacks at any time from dusk through to dawn. Experience allowed him to work with devastating speed so the keepers around knew neither when nor where nor how he would strike. Because he went out almost every night, he had no need to take risks, amass big bags; he could get into a wood, take ten or fifteen pheasants and be off within minutes, knowing that the next night he could do the same thing, and on and on throughout the winter months.

This was where I came in: preparing equipment, spying out the land, picking up birds that had been left beside the wayside and then perhaps peddling them around to sell. Sometimes I would be a lookout, and sometimes I would just go to help Mears or even stay in the cottage at home to field any enquiries made by suspicious policemen. My duties were many and varied, and sometimes I was even allowed into the wood myself.

I can remember the huge numbers of birds, rabbits and hares that passed through our eager hands, and I have no doubt that Shino, Mears and I caused a great deal of frustration and anger in the course of that particular year or so. There were, however, limits to our activities. Shino, for example, could be ruthless and was not afraid of fights. Nevertheless, a black eye, a broken tooth or a bloodied nose was one thing, but Shino would never, ever, dream of doing permanent injury to a man any more than he would to the countryside that he understood intimately and loved totally. To Shino, poaching was a profession every bit as much as his worm-digging, but it was not something he wanted to abuse, at least not the way he looked at things. His motivation puzzles me today, although I took it for granted then; he was certainly never short of money, for worm-digging paid well and went virtually untaxed. The money that Shino made from his night trade would just as often be given away here or there around the village as actually spent upon himself. It would be easy to say that it was excitement that Shino craved, and certainly when we crept through a silent, moon-gleaming wood my heart would beat like a drum: Shino, though, would be just as cool as if we were walking out in the morning over the mudflats with our forks on our shoulders. Even if things became sticky, even if we were chased, Shino showed little emotion, never mind fear. Afterwards he might laugh about it in a short, boisterous way, but immediately it would be life as usual.

I have come to think that Shino was a naturalist of a rather individual sort. Poaching allowed him to pit his wits against nature in a most direct and gripping fashion. Keepers would probably disagree with this, but a good poacher is probably more at home in a wood than any other human being, and that was what Shino loved so much. There was also the added satisfaction of outwitting the gamekeepers – one of them in particular – who are no slouches when it comes to the ways of the country, and Shino certainly relished these long-term duels with men that he could read as minutely as a pheasant, a deer or a sea trout.

It is easy to understand why, for over a year, I was so totally mesmerized by this tall, charismatic countryman. My ageing and respectable parents were horrified that I should adopt such a figure as a rôle model. My father was a lawyer in the area and they both regarded this relationship as the ultimate rebellion of sixties youth, and began to wonder seriously if my education would ever be put to worthwhile use. Great was the tension between us in those days, never more so than when I was caught creeping home at dawn, plastered in mud, bracken and twigs, bloodied feathers still on my hands and quite exhausted from a night under the stars. God knows the threats, the warnings and the inducements they threw my way at those times, but leaving Shino was an impossibility for me.

13

Foxes will point out the difference between the poacher and an ordinary mortal in the countryside more than any other creature. The normal person walking through woodland may possibly see a fox once or twice, or never in his whole life. The poacher, on the other hand, not only sees foxes most times he goes out, but probably knows to within an animal or two the exact fox population of his area. He will also know individual foxes by sight. This is simply because the poacher and the fox operate along the same sort of lines and can both move as quietly and unobtrusively as each other. The poacher thinks like a fox and is able to merge into the countryside in an almost surreal way.

He was larger than life, full of generosity, of humour and of wit, and above all a mine of the sort of wisdom I have always worshipped. Apart from that period of study I had always lived in the country and had wanted to absorb every single thing about nature; but only when I met Shino did I realize that I knew nothing at all. Life with him was a constant, blissful education: things that I had been deaf to, now barked at me as loud as a dog fox; things I had overlooked were now as plain as the noonday sun. The countryside puzzle started to fit together piece by piece into a rapidly completing jigsaw, and I was happier than I had ever been in my life before. This was no rebellion, but rather my coming of age in the countryside, and even though our ways parted, I still thank Shino immensely for everything he taught me. Although now I regret the cloud that that year placed over my relationship with my parents, I can never regret any single night under the moon in a wood with Shino.

2

Shino and His Friends

'*T*wo owd boys pays up for a boot to goo fishin' in. I dunno whar exact it war but they started orf an' ad their owd rods over the side. First orf they caught northing so George, he say "Joo," he say, "not doin too good, are we boy?" "Lord no we haint. Thass a rum 'un. Best we goo on."

So they puts the owd rods in t' boot an' they goo 'arf a mile and 'ad another go thar wi' their rods, do yer see? Blast, they 'ad a hell o' a lot o' fish – tharty at list – an' put 'em all in the boot.

"Joo," say George, "'tis a grand place 'ere an' no mistake." "'Tis too," say Joo, "we mun mark the place so we git back 'ere in mornin'!"

So Joo he push the fish orf an' he take a bit o' chalk out o' 'is pocket and draws a gret owd cross on t' bottom o' the boot. Anyways, they carries on wi' the fishing for 'arf an hour an' it started to git dark an' George he say, "Joo, it's getting cold an' dark."

"Aye, boy," says Joo, so they tek the rods in and aways they goo back to the bank. They're a tekkin the stuff out

15

an' owd George he say, "Joo, hev we marked that spot then, loike oi sed?"

"That I 'av owd partner," says Joo, and he pushes the tharty fish orf and he show George the cross.

"Blast," say George, "Joo, you're a pore owd fool!"

"Why?" say Joo.

"Why," say George, "'cos we might not get the same boot tomorrer!'"

So went one of Tip Up's favourite tales of Shino's father, Joe, and his old fishing partner, George. The dialect is certainly not easy and there are some strangers who never really come to understand it properly; certainly for reading it does make heavy going, and for the rest of this book it made sense to put most of the speeches into something like recognizable English. Another problem with writing dialogue down is that it tends to make Shino and his friends seem like simple turnip-heads, which indeed none of them were. The concept that so many townspeople have of the slow old country boy could not be further from the truth and it would be wrong to reinforce it with too much quaint dialogue that does no real justice to minds that are as sharp as razors!

This is a portrait not of Shino's father, but of his grandfather, all dressed up in his Sunday finery. It is important to realize that poaching was regarded as an honourable way of life by every member of Shino's family, and the great poachers of the past were looked up to as honourable men.

Shino was just one of a whole race of people living on their wits, off the land, in any way they could. There was a great network of men along the coast, in the fields, woods and villages, who kept their ears, eyes and greatcoat pockets open, men who registered the call of every cock pheasant, the retort of every distant gun and who knew the owner of every tyre track or bootprint in the vicinity. Many of these men were diggers, most of them were poachers and all of them made a precarious living from what the countryside had to offer: men such as Nobby Johnsdone, Nick Smith, Crocky Cook, Percy Wilson, Curly Hayes, Stumpy Reed and Choppy Lambert, all men with nets in their sheds, shotguns under their staircases and torches at the ready.

Caw Caw was typical: in the summertime he worked as a small farmer on just a few acres; in the evenings he took a job as a waiter, dressed up as smart as you like with bow-tie and a smile for everyone at the hotel on the quayside. Winter, though, was quite different: the dinner jacket was put away and out came the big coat and the shotgun. Caw Caw was a man renowned for his plentiful changes of clothing and several old bikes, all stashed here and there around his territory, in hollow trees and in deserted barns, all ready for quick changes if he saw policemen about and wanted to keep a low and disguised profile.

Mears, however, was Shino's most frequent companion and there was a deep affection between the two, although they would never allow this to show on the surface. It was an affection that had grown out of trust and admiration: they recognized in each other virtually unfathomable resources of strength and ingenuity. Shino was unquestionably the boss, somewhat older than Mears and with more knowledge and experience; and of course he was the one who bore the 'Shino' name, greatly respected in poaching circles throughout the entire area. Mears was tall, well over six feet, but he still wasn't as tall as Shino. Mears was also massively strong, but even he would baulk at lifting some of the weights we saw Shino move with ease and toss almost casually over his shoulder. It was said that Mears never panicked once, never lost his head; but even so, it was always Shino who took the lead and got us all out of trouble.

There was a huge freedom in their relationship; never once was there any question of dispute over money, for example, or what the night's strategy should be. It was just the same when digging for worms on the morning tide: if Mears was feeling a bit down, then Shino would chip in with a few hundred worms to make up his money. Should Shino want to be away from the muds early for some reason, then Mears would never hesitate to carry off Shino's worms along with his own.

Nor was this generosity of spirit reserved for themselves and poachers alone; they both had the highest regard for some of the keepers. For example, Mr Gee was particularly highly respected. He was a keeper of the old school, invariably well dressed and courteous, even when making an arrest, and had been a keeper on the same estates for over forty years. He knew every rabbiter in the district, and he would make it a rule to stop them all on various occasions throughout the year, and try to direct them to a better life. 'Shino', he would say, 'You know you'd be better off by far if you went to church on a Sunday instead of coming round these roads in search of rabbits. Take heed of my advice, young man, and think of your soul!' Just for those caring words, Shino and Mears would never do Gee's woods at night, for they knew him for a gentleman and would have hated to have done him harm.

In general their relationship with policemen was not a bad one either, not even when Shino was caught by Peggers, the local constable, after a night with the pheasants. This had taken place some years previously, before Peggers had become a sergeant and when Shino was still something of an apprentice at the trade. The poacher was coming round the corner of the rectory wall when Peggers leapt out in front of him, hand up, pulling him to a halt. Shino ducked down, desperately trying to hide the 4.10, but it was no use

It is important to realize that gamekeepers have always been strongly backed up by the law when it comes to poaching. After all, taking pheasants is stealing and is a crime against another's property. It costs a tremendous amount to breed a pheasant, far more than is ever realized at the game dealers.

for the policeman's torch beam was already playing along it, and on the six pheasants hanging from his belt. 'All right, Shino, you'll hear about this,' said Peggers. 'Now be off with you tonight, and we'll speak soon.' The hearing took place in the local town and Shino was fined forty pounds, virtually a month's wages or thereabouts, anyway a good bit for six pheasants; and worse, the gun was confiscated. It was all annoying and humiliating to a certain degree yet predictable: but Shino forgot all about it as soon as he left the courthouse. Then *The Chronicle* came out, and it was shown to him down in *The Admiral*, when he walked the streets, and just about everywhere else he went: in bold letters, the front page screamed out 'Worm-Digger Fined – Raised Gun to Shoot Policeman'.

Shino went looking for Peggers, and found him down in his greenhouse: 'Well, officer, you've made yourself look a brave man and no mistake. You and me will have words about this Wild West story.' Peggers pulled Shino in off the the garden path. 'I know, Shino, but you see, I'm up for promotion and I thought a story like this would do me a bit of good. I owe you one now, old boy, and I know it. I'll turn a blind eye or two on a few nights to come if you let all this pass. Come on man, we all have to live together, you know, and I'd like to think you can help me out on this one.' It was never in Shino's nature to bear a grudge, or to do a man down if he could avoid it, and so the two of them shook hands and he went off laughing.

This is not how things were with Jervis, head keeper at the Bay Meadow estate. Jervis came from a keeper's family, just as Shino came from a nest of poachers, and the gulf between them was set from boyhood. It was as though they had both been born to their particular tasks and were fated to be locked in opposition and loathing for the rest of their lives. Certainly the antipathy had begun when they were children, fighting almost constantly in the school playground, in the street and in the woods. Jervis had been a bully as a boy, and although Shino was two years younger he had always been prepared to stand up against him. One day, when he was only three or four years old, he had gone back to the cottage crying· and his father had got him down on the carpet and shown him how to use his fists. The very next day, the story goes, Shino got to the playground and gave the unsuspecting Jervis a good thrashing. That, anyway, is Shino's version.

Jervis went through his school career arrogant and boastful, confident in the knowledge that his job at Bay Meadow was assured by his uncle, head keeper there before him. Shino never had this security and all he could do was begin helping his father from the age of six or seven. Soon he could pluck a pheasant, skin a hare and even make up a cartridge. By their teens, the future struggles of the two men were clearly laid out: their paths had been chosen by destiny and they had shown themselves more than willing to follow

The means of retaliation open to a gamekeeper in the late twentieth century are strictly limited, certainly when compared with eighteenth-century techniques. Obviously the man-trap is a thing of the far distant past, and nowadays gamekeepers are restricted to owning mean-looking dogs or various alarm devices. A minor deterrent is to place sticks like this one across pathways which are meant to haul down the unsuspecting poacher at night. Generally these are pretty innocuous, but if a gun is being carried with the safety catch off ...

them. They knew everything about each other through constant, apprehensive vigilance. The old saying was that they could recognize each other at two hundred yards on a foggy night, through a dense wood. They certainly knew the exact length of each other's stride, and each other's scent if it hung around in a sheltered dell or thick bracken. Shino could pick up Jervis' coarse, dry cough over half a mile away, and just the sight of Shino's tall, erect profile in the dusk would make Jervis' teeth grind.

Jervis was the only person that Shino ever truly, wholly disliked, for by and large his nature was a warm and open one. Jervis, though, he just could not abide, and over the years the dislike grew at times into a deep hatred. For his part, Jervis always abhorred Shino, ever since the first thrashing in the school yard. His uncle had taught him to despise poachers and treat them as wretches, and yet here he saw Shino liked and admired by virtually everyone in the village. He saw him grow tall, blond and handsome, pursued by all the girls in the class. He witnessed him grow up to make a good living – often at the expense of his own estate – and found himself almost invariably unable to do anything about it. Jealousy and resentment mixed and grew and festered, and Jervis himself said that he would never pull Shino out of the sea, even if he saw him on the point of drowning.

Jervis, by comparison, was a soured and mean-minded man, and there was a whole world of difference in the degree of their popularity around the village. It is true that, to a certain extent, it is the keeper's job to stay aloof from the locals, not to be seen in the pub, and to maintain a distance and a dignity in keeping with the maintaining of law and order. Jervis, however, overdid the part totally, and his overbearing, aggressive ways just seemed to increase with age. It was well known that Jervis was only ever pleasant when he wanted something, and then his manner became condescending and patronizing. This was disliked by the wide-eyed locals even more than his usual curtness.

Shino, though, was all things to virtually all men, and this manifested itself often in many little ways. Mr Barrett, for example, used to own the shoe shop in a very small town, and for over twenty years always informed Shino when Jervis changed his boots. That way the poacher would be able to recognize the new pattern in the woods without difficulty. Then there was the postman, Pip, who would tell him unerringly if Jervis was to be seen unusually frequently on any part of his rounds. The road-menders, the milk men and the farm labourers would all do the same, and even the local doctor and the reverend vicar would help Shino if they possibly could.

The local farmers refused to take sides openly. They knew exactly what Shino had from their own woods, streams and hedgerows over the course of the year, but they balanced that against his willingness to rid them of foxes or moles or suchlike pests, and so never went out of their way to persecute him. They would all, without exception, take a drink from him in *The Admiral* if they met, and would even accept a bottle of whisky now and again at Christmas as an unspoken payment for the offences they had ignored.

Jervis knew about all this, and it irritated him beyond all reason, especially when his uncle retired and he, in his turn, became head keeper. Jervis then did everything possible to put pressure on the local farmers so that they could present a united front to the poacher; but it was no use. These were independently minded men, and they knew Jervis for the bully that he was. Jervis did not even get the support from Bay Meadow that he might have expected: the old squire, it was sadly admitted, was rapidly losing his grip on things. No one would come right out and say the old man was going daft, but that, really, was the truth of it; and as a result he rarely backed Jervis up, or come to that, seemed to know exactly who he was, half the time. Worse was the fact that the squire's heir, his nephew, was reputed to be a 'green', a liberal, and even ambivalent towards field sports. It was noticed, when he visited the estate, that he rarely, if ever, talked to Jervis and showed absolutely no interest in the pheasant-rearing side of the business. He was far more concerned with talking to the forester about plantations, or with the tenant farmers about crops and what could be done for the wild flowers. In short, Jervis knew that he was pretty well alone in his battles against Shino – and this only intensified his hostility and his ruthless desire to see the poacher done away with.

Shino was one of an enormous family, and looking at the tiny cottage of his parents it was difficult to calculate how they had all fitted physically inside. So it was with great relief that Shino had moved out, when he was only twenty or so, and for the last ten or a dozen years had lived pretty much always on his own. Occasionally a girl had come and gone, or perhaps a brother or sister who needed help; but after his over-crowded upbringing it was not surprising that Shino needed, and maintained his own space. There had never been much talk of Shino and marriage, and the only possibility that had ever been was Polly. This quite lovely girl had not been born in the village but had come there as a young teenager when her father had bought a local farm. She had started attending the school when Shino was about to leave, and had fallen instantly in love with him, the big, blond, protective prefect who seemed to laugh so freely with everyone, pupils and teachers alike. In those days Shino only saw Polly as a truly beautiful young girl, one with a foreign-sounding accent and a well-off father. Never once did it occur to him then that she could, or would, have any real feelings for him. However, it was noticed by many at school that Polly always tried to be near him, and in the holidays she would haunt the quayside or the creeks where he might be digging worms or laying nets or sailing his boat. Shino would laugh or talk with her in a brotherly fashion, and she would then go home and cry herself asleep in her bed.

3

Shino's Land

S ome ruinous changes have taken place over the last twenty-five years in England as a whole, and in the eastern counties in particular. Here the population has more than doubled, the number of cars on the roads has trebled, and large lorry traffic has become a serious menace. Hamlets have become villages; villages, towns; and towns often sprawling infant cities. However, these invasions of late twentieth-century life have left Shino's own special world very largely untouched, and there are two major reasons for this.

Firstly, the world that Shino knew so intimately was one of country estates. Shino's village was – and is – fenced, protected on three sides by these large tracts of land that are still under the control of their traditional family owners. Almost invariably these estates date back to the sixteenth and seventeenth centuries, but it was in the eighteenth that they really began to take their present-day form. From the middle years of that century, old houses were pulled down or added to and a veritable building mania swept the area. Parklands, woodlands, lakes, even whole landscapes were built around new, fine houses as rich men really did begin to fashion their own paradise on earth.

This glory, built on the back of successful farming and even more successful politicking, has managed to linger on until the present day despite all manner of problems. World wars, farming depressions and the spiralling costs of labour and never-ending taxation have all threatened to reduce these country seats to rubble, but somehow most of the owners have hung on, kept their inheritance intact and repulsed the destructive onset of progress. As a result Shino's world still survives pretty well intact and would be almost recognizable to any eighteenth-century squire. And it is good that the estates have survived because they are fine places: wonderful mansions with vast porches, mellow, red-brick facades, turreted gables, mullioned windows, lilied moats, and the well-sited ha-has.

Around them, frequently screened by miles of high flint walls, whole communities were built, ringing to the sounds of bell-towers, the clattering of hooves in the stable-yards, the bustle of keeper's cottages and the bees in the honeysuckle which cloaks the old lodges. In the walled gardens, the long-established asparagus beds and stately vines are still cared for, and the beehives are buried in the orchards. The dovecotes are still tended, the summerhouses painted and enjoyed, and in the long meadow grass the horses and the cows are plagued by the summer flies. The hedgerows of yew and privet are still clipped, and the fruit trees and the limes pleached; the ancient oaks in the great deer parks still stand, although new plantations have been established all around them. So although the world has changed, although the life of the twentieth century has hammered at their walls and gates, many aspects of Shino's world still survive, independent, protected through the family line.

All these estates have their lakes, designed and built for future beauty, moon-shaped sheets of water with willowed islands that weep in the breeze, old boathouses, thatch reflections in the water, red-brick dam walls and legions of reeds that light up in the setting sun as if on fire. They hold

Hawks are making a strong comeback throughout the English countryside after a disastrous time in the 1960s when dieldrin and the use of other chemicals on the land were destroying vast numbers of eggs and birds. In many ways the reappearance of the peregrine, sparrow-hawk and the rest is very welcome, and certainly these magnificent birds do a great deal to enhance any country scene. However, it cannot be denied that these big, competent predators do cut a great swathe through the small songbird population, and they are not, therefore, universally welcomed.

tench, smooth-skinned olive fish that jump like porpoises at dusk, and also rudd that glow golden-scaled with fins of flame; some have carp which grow as large as pigs, wallow in the silt and weed for over half a century of their lives. There are perch that bristle and fight and bite on the worms dangled by the estate children; bream as big as dustbins, and pike that keepers swear can swallow a goose.

And then there are the woods, the copses and the coverts, with neatly trimmed avenues and brambles beaten back. Stand on the top of the downs in summertime and you look down on a whole world of green swamping the yellow of the cornfields. Those woods are life itself to the foresters, to the keepers, and of course to any poacher as serious as Shino himself.

Of all the estates, Bay Meadow was the closest and the grandest, reaching right to the boundaries of the village itself. In its prime this domain comprised 25,000 acres, with over twenty-seven farms and employing an army of labourers and retainers; in the late nineteenth century forty men, women and youths had worked in the Hall, which was so vast that it ran its own internal postal service.

The pheasants of Bay Meadow had been prized for a hundred years, and in the 1880s, fourteen keepers and under-keepers had ensured that every shoot was a classic, and that record bags were always there for the taking. Obviously, conditions at Bay Meadow have changed since its heyday, but not enormously so; the aura of magnificence still lingers, the estates grandeur protected by seemingly limitless fortunes.

There is another reason why this region remains so enchanted, so unspoilt, with such powerful sights and scents of the past: on its fourth side Shino's land is bordered by the sea, and no one yet has managed to pour concrete on that. For those who do not know it, this seascape is not a dramatic one of blazing white cliffs, dancing blue seas, and crashing white breakers. It is more subtle than that: a great grey and green coastline where the marsh-head, hazed blue with lavender, slips silently into the sea; a coastline of mists, of quiet tides, of creeks and mudflats, of rivers twisting their way through the marsh under the shadows of the windmills.

In winter, however, the sea often throws down its gauntlet and provides all the drama anybody could wish. When the wind comes from the north, everybody in Shino's land knows about it; they say there is nothing between that coast and the North Pole, that an iceberg or a great white bear could appear on any January night. With high tide and a hurricane wind, the sea flings itself at the shingle defences; the rivers back up and flood their valleys and without delay sandbags appear at cottage doorways. In 1953 a gale combined with a spring tide so the defences were breached and the sea rushed in; houses were destroyed, ships were carried two miles inland, people and livestock had to be rescued or were lost; this is still a night remembered with fear and distress, held up as a warning to anyone who has the temerity to develop this uncertain land.

Shino's village had its great days many years ago, long before its harbour began to silt up and its life-blood was lost.

As a seaport, it was the home of many Dutch merchants and was rich enough to despatch two tall ships to the Crusades. In the twentieth century life is quieter, and it is sailing dinghies and crab boats that are tied up to the quayside now, waiting for the tide to seep in over the sands. An old guild-hall is tucked into the hillside facing the quay, built of Flemish bricks that were beaten out by hand. Along two streets, old houses climb towards the church standing amongst trees, on a hilltop a hundred feet above the level of the sea. Its fine west tower rises a hundred feet higher still, and a slender tower at its north-east corner still shines out a beacon light to guide those alone at sea in the night.

Off these streets lie the old brick and flint houses of the seamen of old, huddled down their own mazed courtyards. The sea can be seen from every bedroom window, so the prospects for the day can be gauged upon rising. Down at the end of one of these courtyards Shino's cottage is still to be found with its low, beamed roof, its shadowed windows and its huge, open fireplace that would belch out heat on a winter's night when we came home frozen to the bone. Then, it was as untamed a house as I have ever entered, with boots and bottles and breeches everywhere on the floor; rabbits in the kitchen, pheasants under the stairs, traps on the table and snares and cartridges and guns wherever you looked; deers' antlers piled in a corner. A stuffed badger by the sink, the mask of a fox on the door and an old otter's tail dangling from a lightswitch. Money lying around in the kitchen, in tins, in drawers and on the floor; the dog's bowl, the milk for the cat and a freshly gutted cod for the fishmonger. Outside were Shino's sheds, with padlocks on them like buttons down a shirt, a vegetable patch irregularly tended, and last of all, an ornate old kennel with its own tidy run.

There were four more houses in the yard, and Shino's was the last; they were formerly a row of seamen's cottages, built when the village was a bustling port. The yard led on to the narrow, crooked high street which dropped away rapidly to

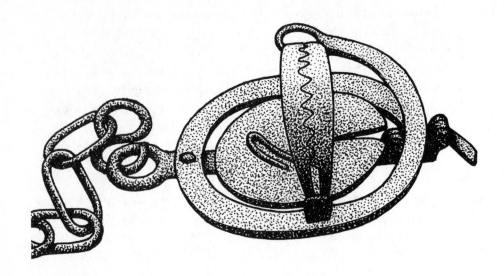

This is a pole-trap, long since illegal. However, it is lethal for pheasants if some sort of bait is put on it. A great many trap designs have been made illegal in the course of the twentieth century, and with good reason: many did not kill outright but simply kept an animal maimed and suffering, alive in torment for hours, if not days, until a keeper came to release it and put it out of its misery. Also, many of these traps are not at all selective, and any passing creature or bird might be caught purely by accident. Shino's attitude towards traps was generally one of distaste; he much preferred actually to see the bird or animal that he was pursuing, and made sure that the whole job was done in as tidy a way as possible.

the quay and beyond that lay the seemingly endless mud-flats. A little way up from the quay on the left-hand side stood *The Admiral*, a haunt of sailors for centuries; goodness knows how many of them, along with smugglers and other scoundrels, had filed into its low-ceilinged, smoky rooms in the past. Little had changed at *The Admiral* for decades, prob-ably because it still remained in the hands of a long line of family owners. There was no heating except for two vast fireplaces, and Walter, the landlord in those days, knew for a fact that all the tables and chairs had been put in by his great-grandfather way back in the last century. No fancy food was served there, but sandwiches like doorstops, good beer in pewter tankards, and closing times as flexible as the tides themselves.

The village is served by two roads: one snakes away along the coast, past the cottage where Mears lived, and on to the mill and old Mrs Crowe, the safe house after many an evening's work; the other runs inland, up past the church, the Rectory and then on to the old roadman's cottage. From there it twists and turns still another two miles before reaching the gate of the Bay Meadow estate itself, with its massive stone arch and high flint walls. Within those walls, in a house on a hill surrounded by trees, lived Jervis, head keeper there, and Shino's long-time, sworn enemy.

4

To Be a Poacher

S trip away the romance and the life of the professional
poacher is a hard and taxing one, especially if, as it was
for Shino, it is combined with a gruelling daytime job.
In many ways, worm-digging could not have been a more difficult occupation to marry to poaching: the season between
October and March is the very hardest for the digger because
that is when the demand for worms rockets, and this, of
course, coincides exactly with the pheasant season between
October and the end of January; and as if that wasn't enough,
rabbits and hares are generally then at their best too – certainly before the latter start boxing and before they all start
producing their young.

Winter, then, was an extremely active time for Shino, especially when you consider that he spent time cutting reeds for
the thatchers just before and after Christmas. In fact when
the days were short, he would seem to work as much in the
dark as in the daylight, often awake for digging at four
o'clock in the morning, not having got to bed, tired from the
woods, much before two. It is true that he might well have
finished digging before lunchtime, but then, of course,

One particularly remarkable lesson the poacher can teach is how to really use the eyes, with a hawk-like scanning of the ground and the sky. So many people walk in the countryside with only a blurred vision of what is around them. For example, it is quite possible to walk to within a few feet of a crouching hare and never guess at its existence. The same can be said of a pheasant nestled in the bracken, or even a little roe deer deep in long grass, only its ears twitching from time to time giving it away. There is so much more life in the countryside than the casual walker realizes.

there would always be a pike or two to be caught, some pigeons to be shot, or the duck-flight to be prepared. In truth, Shino used to say, life was never dull, and how he managed to fit in a more-than-vivid social life was beyond everyone who knew him.

Sometime around April, the worm-digging would begin to slacken off, and game would be out of season; but then the summer demands began to accumulate, and the list was generally very long indeed: Shino was never one to refuse a helping hand to a farmer, perhaps a little sugar-beet hoeing or some picking in the strawberry fields. And from the spring onwards, the eels began to move in all the lakes and ponds, begging to be caught, and off the coast the crabs and lobsters would be about and his boat and pots had to be made ready. Then in July, August and September came the real glory: the sea trout would begin to run the beaches and the estuary, and they could not possibly be missed.

So, winter and summer alike, Shino was sure to be busy, especially when you also take into account the many bonuses that were always appearing to a man with the eye of a magpie. Perhaps it was a goose that had flown into a power-line or a deer that was raiding a farmer's potato field and needed to be stalked. Once he even supplied a zoologist with adders, caught on the heathland, all snared with little loops of wire. Home, as you will understand, was simply a place to hang a hat, to drop a head on a pillow for a short snooze before starting out again.

There can be no doubt that in Shino all the physical gifts needed by a poacher were honed to perfection. His eyesight especially was extraordinary. He could, for example, identify a hawk where most men would have trouble seeing the bird at all. On the mudflats he could name a digger over a mile away in almost impossible light. In fact, if there was any gleam whatsoever in the sky Shino's eyes were trained to take it in and use it to best effect. Remember that one of the greatest skills of the pheasant poacher is to see the bird in a bare tree and get close enough for a shot, and in this Shino excelled. In part this was practice, for goodness knows how many pheasants in how many trees on almost pitch-black nights Shino's eyes had picked out; but there was also a touch of magic in it as well. Even Mears, a poacher for twenty years then himself, could look and look and look into a tree and not see the bird that Shino was aiming for. Something more than eyesight was involved in all this, and if any

The late twentieth century has seen a great decline in the number of gamekeepers: on estates where once upon a time there might have been five or six, now there will be just one; and on small estates it is probably the farmer himself who does a little bit of weekend keepering to keep vermin down. The increased number of magpies in Shino's area are a result of this: in the great days of keepering, magpies and crows were kept severely in check as egg stealers of the highest ability. Of course, it is not just pheasant nests that are raided, but the nests of all songbirds; thus if unchecked, the magpie can become a serious countryside pest.

man had that sixth sense, that unexplained instinct that all hunters possess, Shino had it in plenty.

Co-ordination was another factor, and although Shino was a big man he could move with almost complete stealth. He knew what each limb was doing to absolute perfection, and even blind drunk he would always stoop as he left through the doorway of *The Admiral.* This ability really mattered when he came to the pheasant wood at night if the birds were not to be alarmed, if Jervis and his men were not to be alerted, and if the night were to be a total success.

And of course the really practised poacher must be able to hear as well as a rabbit: often in the wood or meadow at night, Shino would stop and stand stock-still, head inclined to the breeze, and just listen ... Perhaps there would be a bicycle coming down the lane, a door clicking shut on the far side of the wood or a gate creaking on its hinges half a mile away – all sounds that would never even have registered with the ordinary man. His sense of smell was no less keen: if a fox had urinated days before, Shino would pick out the tree. If a man had walked the wood early that day and had smoked a ciga- rette or just washed his hands with soap then Shino would know it; or if a car had passed an hour before, the hint of fuel lying in the roadside grass would be enough to alert him.

Another aspect of his constitution perhaps above all these things was the fact that Shino was very strong, fearsomely strong many would say. Take a normal day in January: he would be up at 4.00 a.m. and walk four miles to the worm beds. Here he would dig for three or four hours, then walk back with the worms and the fork over his shoulder; and yet his day would only be half done. Then he might chop wood, make some snares, cycle out at dusk for some rabbits and peddle thirty or forty of them home in a couple of sacks over his shoulder or tied to the bicycle frame. Even then, he might well have the appetite to patrol in one of Jervis' woods or, if the moon was up and the night was still, perhaps a late night in *The Admiral* bar. Certainly he never saw bed before midnight. It is therefore no wonder that he never carried a spare ounce of fat on him and never had a holiday, not even staying indoors on Christmas Day itself.

To the same degree Shino exhibited all the mental gifts of the top poacher: patience was his hall-mark, despite the pell mell of his life; he would walk the wood, hour upon hour in the freezing cold, never a twig cracking beneath his feet, never once catching his foot in a bramble or a snare set by the keepers. Everything he did was careful, controlled and calculated, every movement was thought out and planned; never once did he rush, thoughtless, into a trap or succumb to an error of his own making.

Stoic, too, was the word for Shino: no matter how wet, how cold, or how hard the wind blew he would never bend before it, either on the mudflats with a fork in his hand or in the woods with his trusty 4.10 at his shoulder. There were nights that I would dread being called out, and mornings when I just could not bear to leave my bed – but Shino would be there, throwing stones at my window, the incredible, remorseless driving force who could not be denied. He knew nothing of weakness, and those around him had to be strong or would be discarded without explanation or sentiment.

What Shino knew, he kept to himself. Never once was he tempted to talk unguardedly in *The Admiral* or to friends, for he knew the inevitability of gossip in country areas. He would be as open as you like about almost every aspect of his life, but when it came to the woods and the night-time then he was like the grave. Never was he tempted into one rash statement, just as he avoided any foolhardy act. No matter how intense the pressure, this mental strength never deserted him. On occasion in the course of his long poaching life the woods would be alive with pursuers, but he would simply sink into the darkness and hide. Or if chased, he kept going, choosing the old forgotten lanes, steadily out-distancing those behind him with calm, measured paces. At these moments of most extreme danger he would keep thinking, keep looking, always totally in charge of the game, ahead of his pursuers, master of himself and the night. On the few occasions that he was caught, it was simply by accident, through a piece of ill-fortune. Sergeant Peggers himself hardly ever planned any reprisals, or any ambush: he simply tried to be out and about as much as possible, hoping that sooner or later their paths would cross in the darkness and there would be something that he would be able to use against the poacher if his luck was in.

Above all, the gift that served Shino the best through year after year of night walking was his total knowledge of the countryside. He seemed to know instinctively when the tide would be on the turn and how fast it would flow. No weather conditions ever caught him out; for example, he could read rain hours away, when it was little more than a haze around the stars. Every sound or action made by bird or animal was interpreted and used for profit or protection. There was nothing that happened in his own piece of countryside that ever remained a puzzle to him for long.

Shino's territory stretched over approximately a hundred square miles and he could be dropped absolutely anywhere within those boundaries, at any time of day or night, and know exactly, to the yard, where he was, which was the best way home and what the alternatives were. He knew every old trackway, every path through the wood or across the marsh. He could avoid every low-slung branch, every tangle of brambles and make unerringly for any gap in the hedge, any old gate in a high brick wall. Shino, in short, could cross a wood as quickly as a deer and be as fast across meadowland as a hare, and the chances of outwitting him or outstripping him were rare indeed.

5

Shino's Teaching

A walk with Shino was like entering a whole new world, where everything was alive and mysteries unravelled. He had the ability to read the tiniest mark on the ground or in the mud and interpret its own fascinating story. He was a good poacher because he was a fine countryman and a true nature detective, the sort of man who looks out at a field or a wood with eyes that see beyond the foliage and the crop, with a piercing gaze that picks out the bare bones of the entire natural world.

On entering a wood, Shino would see exactly where the pigeons had been roosting from the droppings splattered white on the ground beneath. From the wounds on a dead pigeon lying in the avenue he would say with total certainty if it had fallen foul of a hawk, a fox, a badger or a stoat or even if the wind had blown it from the branches and a rat had attacked it as it lay there dying. And talking of fox, no one understood them better than Shino, not Jervis nor any of the keepers around at that time and frequently he would be called in by the owners of small shoots to help them with their problems. The slightest whiff on the breeze and he

If the poacher is going be successful then he must be a true nature detective, capable of reading every single sign that he sees around him. Tracks obviously have to be deciphered, along with droppings, the sight of a kill or even a tuft of fur on a scratching post of fence-wire. Turnips, or any root crops also provide important clues, and a man such as Shino can easily tell whether a particular root has been eaten by a hare or a deer, or even been rubbed around by a badger. Identifying such clues is absolutely essential in building up a total over-view of the countryside and how it works.

A turnip gnawed
by a hare.

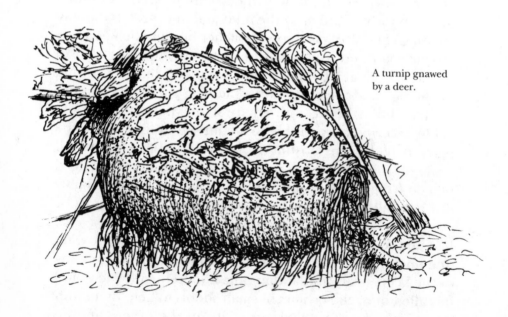

A turnip gnawed
by a deer.

would know where the dog fox had sprayed out its territory, and where he would be likely to find it in the evening, when the light had gone.

On the high sandy ground that overlooked the village, he would know at once if the burrows there belonged to rabbit alone or if a fox had moved in and enlarged them for his own. Badgers were different again, and he would look for the neatly dug entrance, the latrine and the nearby scratching-post. Through the dead and fallen branches Shino would be able to plot the badgers' nightly wanderings, to identify where they had stopped for grubs and bulbs, and where they had overturned the shards of bark to hunt for slugs, worms and woodlice beneath. Here, Brock had scratched his claws on a dead elm, over there dug around for a while at an ants' nest and, exactly on the top of that mole-hill, had sat on his haunches for a good scratch behind the ear; Shino would pick up the tufts of hair still clinging to the long damp grass. It was always a boast of Shino's that he could show anyone their first badger any evening they might care to go out, so sure was he of their routes. Deeper into the wood, a pile of nutshells on the ground would point the way to a squirrel's drey, and a sprinkling of pellets, grey and twisted on the pine needles, would betray a tawny owl sleeping, one eye open, on the branch above.

In the darker regions of wood where the trunks grew closer together, Shino would stop, listen and make not a sound: a hundred yards ahead a branch would suddenly crack as something large moved rapidly away, keeping well hidden throughout its careful flight. Shino would follow through the wood until he broke out into an open field of stubble, and then kneel at once, looking at the soft earth. The print of a red deer would be visible, the soil fresh broken but still no animal to be seen – and you would wonder how such a creature could disappear in so intimate a landscape. But Shino would be scanning the ground, noticing a second print, some broken stubble, a twig freshly bruised, and

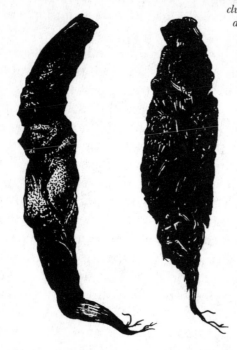

Droppings are probably the most vital clue to the whereabouts and habits of animals. The experienced poacher will know exactly, at a glance, what animal has produced the dropping in question and this could prove absolutely essential to his trade. For example, pheasant and partridge droppings are quite different, as are the droppings of hare and rabbit. If a poacher is called in, as he frequently is, to deal with a troublesome fox, then obviously the droppings will to some extent betray that animal's territory and render it vulnerable to an ambush.

Fox   Badger

would lead the way along the side of the field and point to the ruin of an old kennelman's cottage. There, from amongst the rubble, a big brown head would poke, limpid eyes dancing, nose alive to every scent on the breeze and limbs eternally tensed for flight.

Perhaps some footprints led along the hedgerow: Shino would give them some thought and then pronounce them to be those of Hoppo, the mole catcher and an enthusiastic rabbiter. The prints would turn this way

Tawny Owl

Hare   Rabbit

and that, following the moles' underground runs that linked the hills thrown up on the shaven field. Hoppo's prints might then disappear, where he had in fact followed the line taken by a hare across the field, a track trodden quite bare by its nightly marches to and from its feeding grounds.

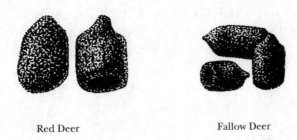

Red Deer   Fallow Deer

Further along the hedgerow, rabbit droppings scattered the dry earth; but Shino was more interested in an area of broken soil where scraps of bloody fur stuck, the scene of a stoat's kill the previous night.

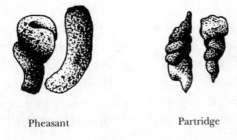

Pheasant   Partridge

The hedge began to drop towards a large dip by a stream. There, water from a storm had run and gathered into a small pond before finally filtering away. A skim of mud was left, and it had become a crazy maze of prints – the heron coming to investigate for toads, the deer picking their way to drink, the badger hoping to stumble on a small rabbit, the pheasants from the wood hoping for a few lobworms, and a fox, in turn, looking for a pre-occupied pheasant. In one part, something had plainly been rolling in the mud, over and over, marking it with great bold heavy strokes as though a deep, coarse paintbrush had been swept backwards and forwards: two young brock badgers had been playing the early evening away.

This field was bounded by a stream, which was crossed by an old and quaking bridge. To Shino it was plain that foxes used this way through the estate; his nose told him that. Beneath the rotting wooden plank the water ran quick and clear and then spilled out into the lake, a stream waving with deep, rich weed, bursting with shrimps, caddis and nymphs. Shino's finger pointed to a trout of about 2lb, rising smugly ten yards beneath the bridge, feeding on gawky daddy-longlegs as they were blown out of the woodland. An alder tree grew the far side of the bridge and towards this Shino inched his way, shielding his eyes with his hands to keep out the light, to see more deeply into the water. Within the roots of the tree a great mottled submarine lay, wickedly toothed, jaws grinning: a pike, well within snaring range, and Shino noted it for the future.

Nor was the lake itself any mystery to him: bubbles rose from the dam wall, tiny pin-prick affairs, the mark of feeding tench. Further out, a huge sheet of water was stained brown where a shoal of bream were on the feed, and to the right the reedbeds were shaking violently as a carp looked for its dinner. A dead fish lay on the bank, stripped clean of flesh, great scales scattered like golden coins; prints led from it to the sluice gate, down the overflow dyke that ran out to the

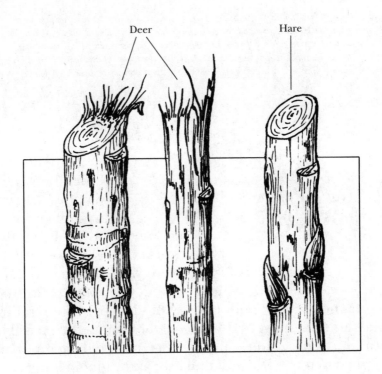

Deer   Hare

The poacher's nature detective-work extends to every single clue that nature provides, including the bitten-off shoots of plants and shrubs. Notice how the hare cuts clean, whereas a deer tends to pull and shred in a less tidy fashion.

sea marshes: to Shino it was obvious that an otter had come in towards the end of the night, and found easy food. Probably the creature had been searching for eels, all fat and silver at that time of year, but undoubtedly was just as happy with this unexpected, fat carpy treat.

The good poacher is also a man who has the necessary technical knowledge and knows exactly what tools are needed for each particular job in hand. Shino's shed was like an emporium for poachers, with goods which had been collected over generations by all the night-workers of the

An otter definitely killed and ate the carp in question: the prints around the dead fish were quite distinctive, as was the way the fish had been almost totally eaten. Mink will often scavenge on a fish killed by a heron, perhaps, but they frequently just pick at the dead fish, leaving a great deal uneaten. Of course, otters can do the same in a playful mood, but generally when they dine they do so thoroughly.

family. Here was piled a veritable poacher's armoury, the tools of the trade stacked high, stored and ready for use at any time. There were four guns, two of them old, but one modern 2.2 and an even newer 4.10, both fitted with silencers. Ammunition lay all around, most of it home-made to suit every possible occasion. There were nylon nets and old hemp nets designed to trap both birds and fish; in the gloom hung clusters of traps, some old, rusted and already illegal, but others neatly oiled and painted and ready for use. There were mole traps in profusion, and snares hung on every nail, glinting like a thousand necklaces in the beads of light. There were boots and hats and gloves, and camouflage clothing that would hide a poacher from the world in snow, on the autumn stubble or in the bare, wintry woods. There were binoculars, torches and lamps from decades long gone, old shovels and forks, buckets and pails, sacks and ropes, and just about every conceivable thing that a man wanting to make a living from the land might ever need.

There was an old shooting stick, leaning against an axe embedded in the wooden floor. Shino pulled it out, dusted it down and opened it up: the antique leather was cracked and peeling but he settled himself on it, outside in the courtyard where the last of the evening sun was dancing.

'This owd stick was my dad's, and he'd often sit on it preaching to me the golden rules of the poaching man. Jervis' uncle used to be head keeper on the estate in those days, and he was no better man than his nephew is now. It's always been in the Shino tradition to work up there every night in the season. The big thing, as my dad used to say, is never to sink into a pattern but always do things different and keep a step ahead. You see, Jervis always expects a man to be working his woods late at night, never just after dark, five or six-ish, and so he's often patrolling around two or three hours after you can be done and gone. And then he gets bored and tired and cold, and shuffles himself off to the cottage around two or three, perhaps; so there's nothing stopping you getting up and hitting the woods again, if you like, just before dawn.

You needn't do a great deal if you're out every night – just half a dozen birds will make it worthwhile some nights, and at other times you might get treble that or more. It all depends on the weather. A big moon's good for seeing birds, but naturally enough they can see you, and if they're aware of one or two of their mates going down, then the whole lot will be up and off and that's the end of things for the night. Far better to wait for a darker night with a bit of wind and that way your approach doesn't get heard, nor your shot, nor the bird going down the tree. But always make sure that you hit the bird clean and kill it outright. Only beginners and idiots go out of their way to wound a bird. As dad always said, if you can't make a clean kill then you shouldn't put your gun up at all. That's what I hate about these modern cowboys that get out and about with air rifles – no damn good for anything, those. And even worse than that are these new crossbows that people are going on about. The chances of a clean kill with one of those are small, and the shaft is always going to be deflected by a branch or a twig. No, give me a 4.10 any night or a 2.2; you just can't beat the old ways.

A moon's not too bad if there's mist on the ground, for at least the birds don't see you nearly as well and you

There cannot be a better shot than the plump pheasant sitting on a bare branch silhouetted by a great full moon. Of course, such a gift does not come along that often, and even then it is double-edged because the brighter the night then obviously the better the pheasants can see the poacher. Also these bright nights are very frequently still, and the sound of the fluttering, falling birds goes a long way towards alarming the whole population of the wood. The remaining pheasants become edgy and nervous, and move away. So a dark windy night is often preferable, especially if the poacher has real talent and knows how to spot his birds in these conditions.

can drop a good few before they know what's going on. And never leave a bird up a tree, hanging there dead, like. If there's a shoot the next day the keeper will just look like an idiot and get told off in front of the guns, and then he'll be even more mad and look out all the harder. I don't mind that much in Jervis' woods, because any harm can come to him as far as I care, but it's still not good practice and I know it. And if you think you're going to make a good bag of birds, don't put them in a sack whatever you do, because they all lie in a heap and get bruised and pulled about. It's far better to lash them to a rope so you can hang them over your shoulder, or both shoulders, come to that, if you're really stacking up a pile – and that, Bingo, is just what we'll be doing tonight!'

6

Lucy

*L*ucy was just about as warm and snuggly a dog as you could possibly imagine, with warm, soft ears and brown eyes that danced with a mixture of merriment and adoration. She also possessed to a fine degree that extraordinary spaniel ability to smile when first seeing a friend, the brown-and-white face creasing into an enormous grin as her entire body cartwheeled around, her little tail a blur of wagginess and the whole performance accompanied by yelps of excitement. Her zest for living was unparalleled, and she always showed interest in every conceivable thing: thus she could never pass any stone or log without investigating what might lie beneath; she would have to smell into every ditch, shed and car boot, sniff at every single gust of wind to know if there was anything worth exploring nearby. Her life was a constant succession of excitements and sensations, and even when asleep she would twitch and paw the air as a riot of dreams fed through her active doggy brain.

Shino made out that he treated her hard, in the true way of a country poaching man, and he also tried hard to decry my own efforts at spoiling her; but in reality, he loved every happy inch of her, and if you were to spy on him when he thought they were alone, their mutual affection would bring tears to your eyes. A poacher, of course, 'has' to have a dog: very many after-dark manoeuvres are simply not possible without one, and for these, Lucy was foot-perfect. Traditionally a lurcher is more usual, but Lucy came from a long line of spaniels brought up to Shino's trade: her mother, Flossie, and her grandmother had both worked for Shino, whilst her great-great-grandmother had belonged to Shino's father; so exactly what was needed from a dog after dark was drilled in so deep that it never really required any formal teaching at all. Shino used to say that Lucy was the perfect after-dark dog when only a few months old. Lucy was four years old then, and husbands were being considered for her so there would be no hiccup in the Shino spaniel line.

For much of a normal day you would never believe that Lucy could work so effectively for her living. In the daylight hours she would be just a daft girl running up and down the yard, following every visitor around with great good humour and trust. Yet even by day she was quite invaluable at finding things – in particular, Shino's car keys, which he was always

Many poachers consider spaniels too flighty to be good companion dogs. Shino did not agree with this, providing the dog was really well trained and came from a good line. Certainly spaniels had run in the Shino family for many generations and the scheme of things was that each succeeding dog be brought up in the poaching way by its parents for two or three years before being considered a fully finished article. Lucy, for example, at that time was about four or five years old and Shino was considering very carefully as to when she should have a puppy and play her part in its upbringing. In the end, she had that puppy when she was six so that by the time she herself was nine or ten and beginning to look forward to a mellow old age, the new dog would take over. That was how the Shino spaniels moved on through the generations.

in the habit of losing. On one occasion he lost them on the mudflats when the tide was coming in: disaster loomed in a very serious way and Mears was dispatched to the cottage for Lucy. Once she was calmed down and her ecstasies channelled into her work, she found them in minutes on the marsh-head; she was treated to half a pint of beer and a ham sandwich at *The Admiral* on the way home.

At night, however, Lucy was an altogether different creature. As the sun began to sink and long shadows threw themselves down her yard, her whole body took on a different texture: tight, controlled and not at all the sloppy old love of a spaniel she had been only two hours before. Once whistled into the van, she would be just a brown smudge in her haste to get on board, and the vehicle would shudder at the power of her leap. Commonly, Shino and Lucy would then be off to a field they had been spying out over the previous few days, one which was away from the main roads and a good distance from farmhouses, and even workers' cottages when at all possible. On arrival, Shino would work quickly: he would attach a long gate-net to trail from the bottom of the field gates along one side of the meadow, and would put his 'yokes' or snares in the 'smeuses' along the same strip of hedgerow. These smeuses are clear for anybody to see: simply well-worn holes in the hedge that hares and rabbits in particular use regularly as they come and go from one field to the next.

Once the net and the yokes had been set, Shino and Lucy would watch the sun finally sink over the marshes which lay to the north, and the sky darken above them from blue through violet to black. They would not stay by the field for this hour or so, but would drive away, call on a friend, walk the sea shore, anything that would not link them with the prepared field. They had to wait for the first of the darkness when the rabbits would come out from their holes and the hares would emerge more boldly onto the field to feed. The confidence of the animals had to be complete: they had to start feeding, forget their fears and begin to enjoy the peace and stillness of the warm night.

Once Shino had judged that the time was right, he and Lucy would drive back to the field; Lucy would be let out at the far end, while Shino drove slowly to the gate and the hedgerow where the traps were all set.

Lucy was magic on these nights. She would make no noise whatsoever, and would be invisible in the soft lights thrown by the moon and stars. When the wind was low you would hear her scurrying here and there, quartering the field, doubling back, sniffing everywhere and occasionally giving out tiny excited yelps but nothing more, certainly never a full-blooded bark. She would move constantly, zig-zagging inexorably down the field where Shino would be waiting in silence, in the darkness and where the traps were set. And if you had your binoculars trained on the field, you would see the grey blobs of the hares lolloping forwards, always a few yards in front of the working dog. Some of them peeled off and got away to the hedgerow and safety, but many found themselves cornered and pushed more and more surely in the direction of the ambush points.

The finale would be over in just a couple of minutes. With his sack on his shoulder, Shino would empty two or three animals from the loose ends of the gate-net, pick a similar number from the yokes and put the sack in the van where Lucy could guard them. Then he would collect up all the tools of his trade, and he and his dog would be off into the darkness with never a look back.

Shino was a great man with snares, his beloved yokes. He made them up himself, simple but deadly devices. A sharpened wooden stick would keep the circular necklace of copper wire in place which is pulled tight under the pressure of a struggling animal, securing it until Shino passed along to inspect. It was the setting of the snares that showed Shino's art, his experience and his complete understanding of animal ways. The height at which the snare was set was the vital thing: one fist high for a rabbit and double that for a hare. Also, you have to know exactly where to set the yokes in the first place: cropped fields are the best, but never where there are sheep or cattle.

For rabbits, Shino would not set the yokes in the hedgerow itself, and any proper examination of the habits of this animal shows why: in the evening, when rabbits first come out, they are very cautious indeed. They will sit in the security of the brambles simply sniffing the wind, stretching, scratching and generally waking up to the new night. If snares were set close in they would feel them, and would never run into them with anything like enough force to be caught. No, a rabbit needs to have built up a little bit of pace for a snare to work at all, so Shino would set them five to ten yards out into the field, placing them across those dimly discernible runs that the animals use on their way into the crop. He was also careful never to leave snares out all night lest the animals should suffer unduly. They would be placed an hour or two before darkness and then checked two hours later. If there were no rabbits in them then he would pull the snares up and call it quits for the night.

I came to believe nothing was much beyond Lucy, particularly after watching her early one Sunday morning when I was waiting for Shino to come out of his cottage. It was around dawn, and Lucy obviously felt she was quite on her own. She woke up, stretched, yawned, shook herself and began to pace around her pen. She sniffed the air, and realized at once there was something exciting about: in a trice she had loosened the catch with her nose; the door swung open and she slid up the yard sniffing all the while. The third cottage had its downstairs window open, and she hopped onto a water butt, onto the window-sill and then her little brown rump disappeared into the gloom. Two minutes later she was back again, a large, succulent leg of lamb in her mouth. She took this back down the yard towards her pen but veered left, slid into Shino's vegetable patch and ate it there, very quietly until all that was left was a large bone. She picked this up,

A great many creatures have remarkably well-formed habits. Hares are a perfect example of this and they will generally travel along the same pathways through crops night after night. Of course these pathways become more pronounced as deer and foxes also pick them out and wear them down even more. In short, these deer highways are a giveaway to a poacher who knows exactly where his snares may be laid.

moved to a patch of waste ground and buried it quite deep. She then pawed some grass cuttings over the disturbed earth, trotted back to her pen, pulled the door back with her teeth

Foxes also have very well-defined routes around their territory, and they often patrol exactly the same meadows each night, moving from one field to another through well-used passing points. They are creatures with an extremely highly developed sense of smell and an inborn cunning, so trapping them at these points is not always as easy as one might think or expect.

and slid the catch back with her nose. She yawned again, went back into the kennel and was soon sound asleep once more! When Shino came out to rouse her, she gave every indication of being quite dead to the world.

Into the New Year, when the days were still very short, Lucy fell ill in a terrible way. One evening, as was usual in the winter, she came into the porch for her dinner; she had eaten it quite happily when, suddenly, she was sick. The poor dog looked every bit as alarmed as her master – wide-eyed, shaken and quite obviously feeling rather ashamed. Whining softly, her tail and ears to the ground, she set off without being bidden to her run.

Shino thought little of this until the next day when Lucy's breakfast was treated in a similar fashion, and she now showed definite signs of distress. Still, she looked eager to get out onto the mudflats; but after just half a mile she collapsed, making the most painful wheezing noise which burbled deep down in her chest. It was quite pitiful to see Shino carrying the dog off the marsh, the normally vibrant creature now a sad, flopped-out bundle, just the glimpse of a pink tongue licking her master's cheek and ear.

Her condition did not improve: she had never been one of those fat sorts of spaniel and she lost weight rapidly; after seventy-two hours there was no alternative but to take her to the vet – never, until now, an easy decision with a dog as boisterous as Lucy, but this night she simply lay in Shino's arms accepting everything done to her in the most helpless of ways.

The verdict was as Shino had feared: 'I'm afraid to say that you're exactly right, and that this dog has been poisoned. I don't think at this stage that we're going to find out what exactly has been through her, but it has left a lot of damage, I'm afraid. I don't know what her chances are – no, it's no good looking at me like that – and I think we just have to start praying.'

Shino drove home with tears in his eyes, and Lucy's head laid on his leg. Now she slept in the house, constantly by the fire, and she hardly stirred throughout the rest of the winter. Sometimes the sun streaked through the windows just before midday, and she would get herself to the door and scratch to be let out for a romp in the yard. But invariably this would be a mistake: the dreaded rumbling and grumbling would well up from her lungs and she would begin to totter on her legs and have to roll over on her side, breathing deeply.

All the while Shino followed the vet's advice minutely, preparing soft, bland food that she hardly had to chew and was easy to digest. Sometimes when the spaniel was at her weakest he would prop her up and feed her on a blanket, by the fire, with her own large spoon.

It was a time of deepest anguish, and for days on end Shino hardly left the dog except to dig some worms; then he would get back to the house as quickly as possible, forsaking his poaching and his usual walk by night. The weather was particularly harsh, with heavy winds and almost constant driving rain streaking the windows and rattling the frames. Shino would sit up much of each night with Lucy, stoking the fire and muttering: 'If this dog should die, if she should die, then somebody will answer. I'll tell you, tell you outright, somebody will answer for this dog.' He would reach out, stroke her head, tickle her behind the ear and look into her deep, brown, soulful eyes.

Lucy had always been quite the darling of the village and virtually every day somebody would call offering a titbit, a piece of chicken breast, half a sausage, anything to tempt the poor dog's appetite. As the days slipped by, people began to go away slightly happier, noticing that her tail beat just that little bit more strongly and that there was a gleam more light in her eye.

With everybody, Shino talked over the question of the poison. He could not understand it; he ripped his own shed apart, searching everywhere for anything that he might have mislaid from times past that could have hurt the dog, but there was nothing. He retraced carefully in his mind the period before Lucy's illness: at that particular time the weather had been very cold and everything had been frozen hard, so there was absolutely no chance that the dog had taken contaminated water from some tyre-track in a field somewhere. The more he thought about it, the more he felt sure that the dog had almost certainly been poisoned on purpose, but by whom? But there was no proof, and he was urged to be cautious.

'Shino, you've just got to be careful, man,' said Mears. 'We know how it is between you and Jervis but you can't prove anything and until you can you'd better not say anything.'

'I'm not saying anything,' replied Shino, 'but you know, Mears, as well as I do that the bastard's mother was ill just before Lucy collapsed, and that he'd been round here for the first time in years. If that's not coincidence, then what is?'

It was true, Jervis' mother did live just across from Shino's yard in a cottage on the far side of the street, and she had been ill during the week leading up to Lucy's collapse. Jervis, most unusually for him, had actually come to visit, and he could easily have left behind a contaminated present for the dog. But it didn't bear thinking about: we all knew about Jervis, but surely not even he would stoop to that.

In late February it was decided that Lucy was just well enough to go out on the marsh, the first time for something like seven weeks. It was a careful, guarded affair and all the diggers watched with apprehension and hope intermingled. Once the spaniel did fall, but only because her paw caught in a discarded piece of anchor rope; everybody watching felt an upsurge of relief. And by the spring, Lucy was eating normally again, the sheen had returned to her coat, her eyes were bright, her nose wet and she was working properly; just in time to catch the end of the rabbit season!

The vet himself could only say that her recovery was a minor miracle, and a happy one for all concerned; not least was the fact that it helped maintain the peace between village and estate, for Shino was not the only one to suspect Jervis of foul deeds. And then the conviction that the illness could be laid at the keeper's door was reinforced in the most spectacular of ways. As spring turned into summer Lucy had once more become the lively bundle of her former self; and at this time the agricultural shows started up again. At one particular show the day was bright with high, fleecy clouds; the crowd swarmed in good humour, and Shino and Lucy were enjoying the hospitality tent of a large gunsmith. Then, two stands away, Shino saw Jervis approaching; he had been alerted by the familiar dry cough, and turned to see the tall, stooping figure he recognized so well. The gingery-haired Hawker was with him, giggling nervously in Jervis' crooked shadow, both of them darting magpie looks here and there at goods on the stalls.

Jervis turned, and his eyes met Shino's: those around went silent and the sudden quiet made Lucy look up from her bowl. Now the figure of Jervis was looming over her, and her hackles began to rise. Stiff-legged, the spaniel walked towards the keeper, a roar mounting like thunder in her throat. Shino watched dumbfounded; to him it was as though the dog were speaking, pointing out the guilty man, the man who had caused her such harm.

'Keep that dog of yours under control or else I'll have it reported and put down, I will. There's twenty witnesses here to what's gone on,' spat Jervis.

'It's what's been gone before that the dog's shown me now,' Shino replied, his voice choking with menace. 'What I've known winter-long has been proved beyond a shadow, and now I can take the action that's due to you.'

Mears tried to pull Shino back, Hawker wrestled a second with Jervis, but then the two men were at each other, punching, kicking and crashing through the tables and surrounding displays. The weight of eight men was needed to pull the keeper and poacher apart and to hold them there. It was a turbulent, noisy stalemate, however, and unseen in the mêleé Lucy crept forwards under a table, right up to Jervis and bit him soundly through the thick stocking into his calf.

A roar went up at that, and so great was Jervis' fury that the battle all but began again; but Hawker was quick to lead the hobbling keeper away. As he looked over his shoulder, his eyes blazing, he saw Shino, shirt ripped, standing in a pool of sunshine, and by his side Lucy, once again drinking from her bowl.

7

Shino's Woman

'*I* will always love him, just as I always have. Even after the things that have happened and the things that were said. I'd have him back today, tomorrow, or next year or absolutely anytime. I know now that he'll never come back to me, but whenever the door-knocker goes, I always jump up and think perhaps, perhaps this time he's coming back for me.'

Polly looked around the shed where the women were drooped over piles of brussels sprouts. The cold in the building was intense and they all sat in their coats, trying to peel the small vegetables as best as they could in gloves, their fingers numbed. Polly's breath hung in the still air and her voice broke the silence. 'I know you all think I'm mad for what I'm saying and I don't blame you. But you must know that while he brought a lot of sadness into my life he's also given me the only true happiness I've ever known, and I'd never regret one single day with him.' The cold afternoon sun looked briefly and bleakly in through the dirt-grimed windows, and then it sank like a balloon deflated after the party. None of the women around Polly said a word, though they wanted to; they all had their own opinions of Shino, many of them had known him well. There certainly wasn't one of them that did not know what had passed between this striking fair-haired woman and the great Viking poacher.

After leaving school Polly had flirted with college life, but had been drawn back irresistibly to the village and the man whom she loved so deeply. Not surprisingly, her parents disapproved violently, pleading with her to forge a new life and forget the blond poacher who seemed to avoid romantic entanglements in his life. The girl became more and more distraught, her studies suffered and were finally abandoned altogether, and she retired to work on her father's farm.

This was a dark period for the girl with the golden hair and eyes of an electrifying blue. Her parents' reproaches and Shino's rebuffs drove her finally to a life with Percy, another of the diggers along the coast. Nothing improved. Percy was small and dark, like a gypsy, with a wicked temper and an addiction to alcohol and gambling. It was usual for him to be away for days at a time, and to return without a word of explanation or apology. Finally, during one of these disappearances, Polly went to a party in the village to celebrate the approach of Christmas. The evening was a very merry one with clear frosty skies, and the local people stumbled in from the cold, eager for warmth and excitement. A little before midnight, Shino knocked on the door, pheasants in pocket and Lucy by his side, and he, too, was welcomed in.

By the early hours of that morning, Polly was telling Shino how she had always loved him, and how she even remembered the moment that love had first been kindled, in the playground one September morning eight years before.

Later that same day, the two of them went to Percy's dark, deserted cottage, gathered her few belongings and returned to live together in the village.

Percy was a furious and vengeful man when he returned, hung-over and bankrupted, to find his house cold and empty. There was a furious encounter in the yard outside

Shino's cottage which stopped just short of physical violence but cast a shadow over the happiness of the two young people. Percy threatened a good many things both to their faces there, and later to those who would listen in the village.

Polly's parents visited almost immediately, terrified for their daughter and horrified by the menace they had seen in Percy's black eyes; but although they argued and reasoned, they were bound to fail and Polly stayed with her Shino through Christmas and on into the New Year. For them both, this was a special time and the cottage was bright, warm and happy. Shino went out less at night and when he did, Polly would join him, against his wishes, her long hair falling like a silvered stream under the moon-cold skies.

Tempests in the lives of men are frequently reflected in the heavens – or so country folk say – and a period of very wild weather played backdrop to all these emotional storms. When the skies cleared, hard frosts set in, so extreme that even the mudflats where the river flowed into its estuary were frozen. At first, Shino and his fellow diggers continued to go out at each low tide, but so miserable a number of worms did they collect that at last they gave up and spent most of their days in front of their fires at home or in *The Admiral*. Indeed, as the icy grip continued, the cold became so extreme that the mudflats and the sands froze hard as soon as the tides uncovered them, and any digging was quite futile.

This weather had a dire effect on bird life: small waders became so weak that they were easy prey for the hungry hooded crows and black-backed gulls; Brent geese became completely fearless; and as the marshes remained frozen, most of the moorhens began to die. Marshes and meadows saw a terrible number of deaths: bitterns and herons perished, and water-rails were amongst the first to succumb to the cold – Shino found fifteen dead just where the river moved into the sea. In the little harbour these birds were seen attacking a starving dunlin, and even pecking at the frozen corpse of a coypu. Wrens were frozen to death on the very coldest nights; Shino had forty roosting in a single nesting-box down by the kennels.

All the gardens in the village were invaded by a huge number of redwings, fieldfares and blackbirds which existed on spoilt apples left over from the abundant harvest of the autumn. The people of the village saw all manner of strange sights: a kestrel attacking a woodcock in flight, and a water-rail which had swooned in a coma was found to have its belly feathers encased in ice. It was thawed out and Mears fed it on worms until it accepted them fearlessly from his gnarled fingers. Shino did his best to keep alive three half-starved bitterns, caring for them in a pen and feeding them on sprats. Sykes reported that he had seen a dying mute swan killed and eaten by a fox. Altogether these were trying, frightening times; and there were those who said worse were to come.

However, at long last the frosts became a little less severe, and shortage of money began to push the diggers back to work. Weather like this produces strange phenomena over a land where the sea meets the sky and the shore with never a break. When the muds are frozen and the relatively warm tide retreats exposing the damp sand to the freezing air, an extraordinary thing sometimes happens. As a particular temperature range is reached – often hours later, even as the next tide approaches – an impenetrable mist can fall, so thick that it is impossible to see more than a yard before one's face and even the prongs of the fork can be lost before they bite into the sand. For worm-diggers, this type of weather threatens the terrible danger of getting lost, especially as the fogs are worse in periods of complete calm, when there is no wind to aid direction. Then it is quite possible to become disorientated, and diggers have been known to wander, helpless, out to meet the oncoming sea and their inevitable deaths.

Over the years, all the diggers had come to realize the danger such conditions impose, and had learned to combat it in the most simple of ways: as each man moved over the muds, he would scrape great arrows in the sand that he could

Lugworms are probably the most popular sea-fishing bait and they are also used a great deal by the long-liners who might well go through two or three thousand worms in a single night. As a result, worms are in constant demand, even though most of the English shoreline has been dug to near exhaustion. This means that the diggers have to work very hard for an ever-declining number of worms, and prices rocket. It is a hard, gruelling profession and it can take place in the most frightening of circumstances. A good digger, however, works like a well-oiled machine without pausing or hurrying, simply moving rhythmically through the muds, the bucket ever filling.

follow when the time came to walk off through the fog, should it not lift. This had become the diggers' first rule, and it was an absolute life-saver.

Shino, digging alone as always, had made his own way out from the headland, striking out around six o'clock in the morning, some four hours before the new tide was due. Two or three other diggers saw him go, wending his way over the hard shingle, over a creek where his footsteps merged into oozy nothing. At the limit of their eyesight, they saw him stop to make his first arrow and then he was lost into the nether world of mist, water and shifting sand, where no sound penetrates but the occasional cry of a tern wheeling far above.

Percy, still nourishing his hatred, had watched all this as well from one of the cattle shelters on the marsh – and set out along the same trail, thirty minutes after Shino, when the marsh was quiet and the mist far thicker than before. Shino was digging hard; the temperature was way below freezing but the sand was like a radiator after the warm tide. His coat was thrown off after an hour; four hundred worms in the bucket, and he knew he was going well. Two hours would be his limit: he was anxious about the weather and in no mood to take risks. He was working in a rhythmical way, like a machine, never hurried, never changing his speed or his stance. At times like this the body takes over, with the mind counting the worms, running over life and its problems, and alert always to a change in the breeze or to the light values. The hours passed, the mist thick as cotton-wool and silent as the tomb, and Shino just continued to dig, to fill the pail with the slithering, slimy worms.

Percy followed the arrows for half an hour until he heard Shino digging a hundred yards ahead; the rhythmic thrust of the fork and the swish of falling sand were unmistakable. He stood there a minute, head on one side; and then he walked back the way he had come, carefully rubbing out any of the few footsteps that remained in the sand, both his and Shino's. Shino's arrows, too, were erased, with quick, soft strokes of the boot that left no impression remaining in the grains.

There were nearly one thousand worms in Shino's bucket when he finally stood and straightened. The tide would be on its way, he knew, and so must he. The muds in a mist were no place to linger, and he hoisted the worm bucket onto the prongs of the fork, balanced it on his right shoulder and followed his first three arrows off into the fog. But the fourth arrow he did not find, nor the fifth, nor the sixth, no matter how wide he fanned his search. Truth to tell, in looking he had lost his original three points to safety; he paused; water was already pushing here and there across the sands.

Here the sea runs in no general direction, it simply drifts in from all points of the compass as the tide seeps in, following the various channels and depressions. First a skim of water, like oil, covers the sands, and then it deepens rapidly. Within five minutes, the sea was at Shino's ankles, and then as he wandered, it began to creep up the calves of his boots. The poacher did not panic: that was not his way, and he knew enough of the muds to realize that such a course would inevitably mean death, out there, quite alone, four miles from hard land.

He shouted as loud as he could, and listened, standing stock-still, head inclining this way and that. Nothing. Some men might have felt and feared death, creeping through the mists towards them, but not Shino. The water was at his knees when the faintest breeze began to blow, so shallow that nine out of ten men would have ignored it. It was a cold breeze, and Shino not only noticed this but felt, intuitively, that here was a wind from the north-east. If he made his way directly before it then he would be bound to come to the coastline.

He took his hat off, the better to feel the wind whispering against his neck, and set out, trusting his life, literally, to the wind. In places the water was shallower and his heart leapt, but at other times it deepened considerably, so deep that at times he was even swimming, discarding the fork, the bucket and the worms, following the slightest of ripples on the water ahead of him and always going the way of the breeze.

He came at last to a shallow strand and stood, the water at his thighs, and again shouted, throwing his voice to the strengthening wind. Now, even without straining to hear, a reply came back to him: it was Flossie, Lucy's mother, barking from his van. Now, on the verge of safety, he began to run when he could, knowing that he had yet to tackle the deep black channel before the marshland, a channel that might yet prove too much for him with its erratic, powerful currents. Flossie's barking became louder and louder: the mist was breaking up, and soon he could see the looming outline of the marsh and the dykes, and then even the outline of his vehicle.

The swim across that final channel was shattering to a man who had suffered in the way Shino had, and his strength was totally sapped by the time he finally struck hard ground and staggered, dripping and bleeding, to his van.

Shino arrived back at the cottage, his clothes frozen on him and icicles in his hair. He was in a fever of fury. Polly helped him to bathe and put him by the roaring fire while she listened to the tale of that near-fateful morning. Eventually he dressed and went down to *The Admiral,* pushing open the door of the snug where Percy always spent his winter afternoons.

The digger started up; 'You bastard, you bastard!' he choked before Shino reached him, smashing through tables. The two men fought right through the bar and then down the steps into the street; they rolled past the guildhall and onto the quay. They were still fighting when they were no more than specks out on the muds, which was where Peggers reached them: had he been any later, Percy would have been ripped apart.

Later that night Shino was cautioned and released from the nearest police station; he returned to the cottage to find it in darkness. Polly's father had come for his daughter on hearing the news of the fight and nothing, not begging nor sobbing, would turn his head now. Polly's possessions were again gathered up, and with them she was taken home.

Shino had understood the love of the farmer for his daughter, and he shared it, believing now that he could never offer her the life that a woman deserved. The affair with Percy and its dreadful aftermath left deep scars that he said time would be unable to heal, though I, personally, was not really sure. I knew that though Polly tried over and over to leave the coast and forge a new life, she could not help but return each time after a few weeks or even a month or so. And Shino, though he knew other women, could never settle with them, always finding something missing in them for him, always looking for glimpses of what he once treasured but felt he had lost.

8

Shino and His Pheasants

'Come on Bingo,' Shino said; we were sitting by the lake catching pike, watching the clouds scud by before a wind that was bending the reeds right down to the water's surface. 'We'd best be off to see to Mossy Wood tonight early on, whilst Jervis has his tea. The night's just fine for it, with this wind and all.'

The first weeks of the pheasant season can be difficult for the poacher. The trees are frequently still in leaf, oaks especially, and this gives the birds a great deal of camouflage at night and consequently makes them hard to shoot. Also, in the early days of each season, there are many small, under-developed birds and these are very difficult to make out in the dark of a night wood. But there is great demand for pheasants at this time and so the poacher cannot really let the market go unfulfilled.

I would have liked to have stayed on, because the afternoon had been excellent and the early evening offered every chance of a big fish, but I was the junior partner and dutifully reeled in my tackle. We were soon at his cottage and collected together the 4.10, some cartridges, a couple of ropes to hang the birds on, and of course picked up Lucy, and the three of us then set off in the gloom towards Mossy Wood. Shino and I dismounted from our cycles a mile away, just as the wood was beginning to loom big and black on the crest of the hill. The wind was still as strong, and although there was a moon, the cloud kept racing past it, hiding its face apart from the occasional glimmer.

The three of us entered on the windward side of the wood, and there was a very good reason for that. Pigeons always roost in the far-side woodland belt which is sheltered from the prevailing wind, as far away from any cooling breezes as they can possibly get. That night this sheltered belt was over towards Jervis' cottage; had we gone on that side past the pigeons, they would have gone up in a cloud and the game would have been over right away. With the wind as it was, we could creep in on this side and do what we wanted, and the nearest pigeon would be a good half mile away. The other good thing about it was that if left undisturbed, the pigeon flock would act as an alarm system for *us*, and we could have known at once if either Jervis or Hawker was coming to check the rides.

As usual I was behind Shino, who was moving very carefully and very slowly down the first ride, a stick in his hand, flicking it here and there, feeling for any snares that Jervis might have put out to trap us. Normally, if there was any light in the sky, Shino would not bother with such a precaution but that night it was particularly dark. The big man in front of me stopped and looked up: I don't know if he saw or simply sensed a bird, but the tiny beam of the torch light picked out its flickering eye. Shino moved round slightly so that the wind was blowing over his shoulder and would disguise even

71

On cold nights pheasants will be seen sitting on their perches, their breast feathers covering their toes completely, seemingly trying to keep as warm as possible. On nights like this they might well be found in fir woods, where there is at least a little shelter from the falling frosts.

more the sound of the shot that was to follow. The gun made a dull 'crump' sound and the pheasant was down on the ground, fluttering just a little, but Lucy was on him, quick as an arrow to stop him alarming the rest. The dog knew the game all right, better even than me, and brought the bird straight to my hand as she saw Shino moving slowly on again, down the ride.

Altogether we had twelve birds in a little over twenty minutes. We didn't wound and leave any, nor did we lose a single one. All Shino's spent cartridges were stored in his pocket and we made every attempt to avoid the low, wet patches so that our prints were kept to a minimum. I suppose there must have been a few feathers and perhaps one or two of Lucy's paw marks, but even so, any but the most experienced keeper would have had trouble divining exactly what had happened.

Within minutes we were back at the bicycles and sooner than that, into the cottage, the door locked, the fire stoked up, having a cup of tea before going down to *The Admiral* for the rest of the evening.

That was how Shino liked to work, quickly in and out, taking no real risks whatsoever. Ninety-five birds out of a hundred fell this way – but Shino always kept his eye open, was always looking for something a little bit different, a new challenge, something perhaps to provide a bit of amusement.

For example, later that month he noticed that a dozen or so of Jervis' pheasants had left the estate proper and had begun to roost and feed in the old rectory's orchard, which had fallen into great decay. The birds seemed quite happy in there and had been resident for some while, so the question was, how to get them out? There was no possibility of going in there with a gun because the outlying houses of the village were dotted here and there on all four sides. But inevitably Shino had his own ideas.

I found him sitting at his table, with cardboard and scissors and glue, making little helmet-type affairs, brown cardboard cones about three or four inches high and the same distance in diameter. 'What on earth ...?' I exclaimed. Shino hardly looked up and simply laughed and carried on with his work. Soon there were fourteen or fifteen examples of his handiwork completed on the table.

It was late afternoon by now, and he threw the ropes at me, picked up the cones, fumbled in a cupboard and said that we were off. Lucy was collected from the kennel, put on the lead and off we strolled up the village street.

There were long shadows entering the old orchard when we arrived, and Shino pushed in through the broken-down wall and moved towards one of the larger open areas where he knew the birds came out to feed just before dusk. From his pocket he drew out a large paper bag filled with currants, and began to sprinkle these liberally on the grass. He then bent down and pulled out his cones. From another pocket appeared a jar of treacle, and this he smeared liberally inside each cone. Finally he sprinkled raisins into the cones, making sure that plenty of treacle still remained visible. Then he placed the cones here and there, dotted out widely over the area.

The three of us then retired some way away towards the perimeter of the orchard, and sat down to wait.

The pheasants had been alarmed by our arrival and had hidden themselves, but as soon as we had moved off, they

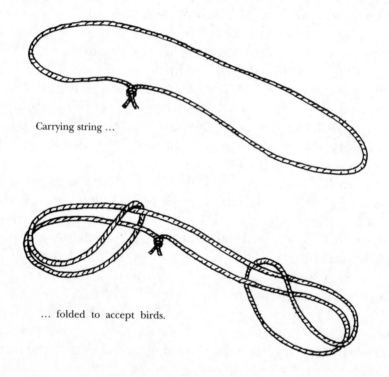

Carrying string ...

... folded to accept birds.

The amateur poacher will probably put his birds in a sack as he gets them. This is all right for two or three birds, but for any greater number, those at the bottom tend to get squashed and will lose condition quickly. The true poacher, the man who knows what he is doing, will carry his birds on strings, made up as the diagram suggests. It is an easy job simply to put the bird's head through the noose pull it tight and put the strap across the shoulder (opposite). A lot of birds can be carried in this way, besides which both hands are then also left free.

Strings in use

came out of the long grasses and began to feed voraciously. They soon found the raisins (Shino had fed a good few to them over the previous days so they were eager and looking for more), and began to feed in earnest. Soon the first had found the cone and had seen the currant inside. It was a cock bird, and he pushed his head down as far as he could, scraping around for the pieces of fruit. But when he lifted his head and tried looking around, he found he was blind to the world: the helmet fitted him as snugly as a glove. Three, five, six, eight birds were similarly hooded, running here and there, colliding, totally blindfolded. Lucy scampered around and did the rest. By the end we had nine birds swinging from our belts, and we simply had to wait for night to fall before moving off and sliding out down the darkness of the street for home again.

To some it might seem a fine dividing line, but there were things that Shino would never do. For example, he detested the practice of leaving currants and corn out on fish hooks, tied to nylon line, only picking up the helpless birds in the morning. It was a trick used by some of the poachers along the coast, but he despised it. Many also liked to hit birds in their cars as they were travelling along the lanes so that they would be stunned and easy to catch. This again incensed Shino, who said that many of the birds were just wounded and managed to get away, only to die in agony up a tree or deep in the long grass. He felt there were certain ways in which no man should behave.

9

Fish Tales

*I*ncreasingly Shino's interest was drawn to the coastline;
he couldn't keep his gaze from it, walking it every day
for his work and whenever he could for his leisure.
Every story of smugglers, pirates, shipwreckers, storms,
underground tunnels, monsters and hobgoblins he lapped
up, and the shoreline became more and more a precious,
unique place the older he grew. The more he thought he
understood it, the more mysteries it seemed to hold for him,
and the more unexplained questions arose. In time he came
to know every pebble and every piece of shingle, every creek,
dune and every last yard of marsh for ten miles east and ten
miles west, just as he knew every wood, meadow, lane and
bridleway up to five miles inland from this treasured coastal
belt. This gave him a land of some one hundred square miles
– more, if you take in the foreshore – which he knew with
total certainty. Yet his sense of geography was strictly limited:
out of this domain he would be utterly, utterly lost.

Storms affected Shino every bit as much as did moons.
Storms. Night storms: the night wind shrieks and piles up a
high tide against the shingle, forcing the river back, ranting

against the sluices, clawing at banking, sliding over the reedbeds towards the cottages. Fearful nights listening to the dancing tiles, sandbags at the door, lamps flickering in the bedrooms, windows rattling to the pulse of the wind-hammering rain.

Storms. Boats blown miles inland. Sandbanks shifted in one night tide. Gulls riding on the gale. 1786 was a date that Shino always talked about, one fixed in his mind by the tales of his father and grandfather: in this year there was an immense late winter storm, so intense that it was as if the hand of God had turned. For two days and two nights the tempest blew, and a vast sturgeon swimming in the North Sea was caught in the turmoil. The enormous fish ran with the rip, and when the danger was passed, found itself in the harbour on the dropping tide.

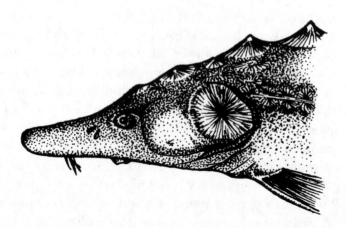

The profile of a sturgeon, the great wanderer of the northern hemisphere. There are many different types of sturgeon, and the one that found its way to the quay on that historic day almost certainly originated from the Baltic or White Sea area where sturgeon were common in times past. These are very big fish, often over 200lb in weight, and they are still maintaining a very precarious existence. The sturgeon's head is an incredible creation: the underneath of that long, pointed snout is riddled with nostrils which give it an extraordinary sense of smell, and those long eel-like barbules are used for probing into the mud, searching out organisms there. What cannot be seen is the huge mouth, situated under the eye; this telescopes out like a great vacuum cleaner, and can suck in a cod in one great gulp.

The fishermen and the merchants were out there, inspecting their damaged boats, pulling them back to anchor and repairing the shattered rigging when they saw the water rise against the force of a great grey-scaled back; a forked tail lashed the steely surface of the harbour, and then the head reared up, hideous with long, pointed nose and writhing barbules. Some of the men ran for their lives, some for the Reverend, and many believed that the hugest storm of their lives had blown the very fish-devil itself to their doors.

Not so Shino's great-grandfather, who had sailed ships to the White Sea and beyond. The stranded leviathan he knew to be a sturgeon, blown in from the Russias as it searched the oceans for herring and krill. Great-grandfather Shino watched the water slip away, revealing the armoured scaling on the fish's sides as it floundered in the sunlight. Then in the ship's dinghy he paddled close to the grounded monster: a single blow to the brain with a boat-hook did the deed, and within minutes the huge fish was lying on the wharf. It measured nearly ten feet from tip to tail, and swinging from the granary beam, weighed in at twenty-eight stones.

Much wood had come down in the storm and the children gathered this together in a great heap on the quayside whilst the men systematically butchered the sturgeon, cutting it into steaks the size of hams. As the light fell, the fire was lit, the smoke curling off to the stars, and the sturgeon was cooked in the flames. The fish fed the village and then its dogs for days afterwards: no caviar was found, but even its innards were used up in the crab pots, though with indifferent results, according to Shino.

No precise record exists of this great event, and perhaps it was Shino's own story. However, there is mention in the parish records of a ferocious storm towards the end of the eighteenth century, and parish accounts point to the capture of a large fish of unknown origin around the same time; so the tale that was always so central to Shino's perceptions of an enchanted coastline could well have some historical basis.

Storms seemed to accompany the family Shino, and they rode them constantly on their path through life. The bizarre tale of Jervis' rainbow trout is a good example of what I mean. Jervis had angered the community by constructing a trout farm on the fringes of the flood-plain. The village was torn by controversy and Shino led the protestations, condemning the plan to divert the river to feed the six huge plastic tanks where the fish were kept. The pure river water was led through an elaborate system of troughs and pipes before re-entering the river muddied and fouled by the mass of trout it was keeping alive. The new squire eventually called for a public meeting; he appealed for calm, and suggested that the farm be given a trial period. This was accepted by most, though predictably not by Shino.

Several times in the trout farm's short life Shino was to be observed wandering around the perimeter before dawn, looking to see if there was anything he could do to hold things back a little, or hamper the keeper's progress. For the poacher had been quite correct, the small river did suffer, even after only one year of the farm's existence. As he predicted, the river flow was reduced, the weeds became choked in a rusty, slimy refuse and the native trout declined as insect life perished. To Shino, this was just another example of Jervis' greed, his oppressive hand over the countryside and his exploitation of the land of his fathers.

Storms, great storms again came to the rescue, to the delight of Shino and, no doubt, that of his ancestors in the churchyard on the hill. Once more the great winds blew from the north and the waters rose, surging over the sluice-gates and onto the river-plain. At night, the meadows drowned and the water trickled, then lapped, then gushed through the perimeter of the trout farm so that by the time dawn broke a crazy sight confronted Shino as he peddled down the lane, Lucy at his side.

The six plastic tanks were bobbing around the meadows: they were like great plastic ducks or bizarre cups floating in

80

a sink, or icebergs cast adrift in a shallow sea; and inside each swam 10,000 captive rainbow trout. The breezes pushed the containers here and there and they wobbled, top-heavy and unstable. They seemed likely to topple at any moment ... surely it needed only the gentlest of helping hands to tip them and let the trout out and on their way. Shino waded out to them and looked inside each: he looked round in the morning light, then found that he hardly needed do any more than blow on them and over they went, one by one, their cargoes leaping as numerous as raindrops over the flooded fields.

Jervis knew Shino had been about – the tyre-tracks in the mud by the gate and Lucy's paw-prints explained that – but the keeper could do nothing: if the entire village had been there to see Shino's part in the rainbows' escape there would have been no witnesses, so great was the bonanza that followed. The herons had a couple of hundred fish, the pike a hundred more, and a few thousand probably got to the coast to be seen no more, down the throats of seals, or who knows, sturgeon! But the rest, perhaps 55,000 or so, nestled in the sea-pool under the shade of the windmill, and there the havoc was wreaked.

Seagulls wheeled in the sky as men and boys from miles around made their way to this fishing frenzy. For a week anglers moved in as anglers moved out. Sometimes twenty would sit around the pool at any one time, each one hooking a rainbow trout within seconds of casting. It was mayhem, with fish leaping and diving and twisting the lines into some vast, unfathomable tangle. And yet hardly anyone went home without a sack of fish for his troubles. Then at night, after the last angler had made his way home, the otters would move in along with the herons; and, at dawn, the flock of cormorants before the anglers appeared once more with their rods, their lines and their cans of worms.

Jervis watched all this from afar, helpless, enraged and embittered. He walked the village street and nearly choked on the smell of cooking trout that came from every window. Morosely he watched the cats fighting for bones and skin around the dustbins. He heard the merriment in the pub and the excitement in the school playground as the child anglers waited for the final bell.

Inevitably, the village became tired of trout, trout and more trout, and even the cats, now fat and sleek, hardly bothered to raise a paw for even the plumpest piece of rainbow. The bonanza was over, and those fish that were left slowly slipped away into the marshland creeks, often to grow on for another three or four years and become veritable silvery giants. Most important of all, however, was the fact that the fish farm was now dead. The six white tanks lay stranded, whale-like, for a few days until the flood-waters seeped away and the lorry came to take them away for ever more. The squire had observed the effects of the farm as clearly as Shino, and the flood had served to avoid a confrontation with his keeper, a man who would have doggedly defended his creation to the last. A new spirit was beginning to guide Bay Meadow into the future.

10

Shino's Summertime

S hino revelled in the summertime; his hair grew blonder and his skin tanned to a golden brown, making his eyes seem an even deeper, more piercing blue. The digging relaxed, poaching took new forms and after the cold days of winter, the warm months seemed designed for happiness. My friend unfolded, purred almost, like some great cat let in from the dark to luxuriate before the fire.

These were long, lazy days and he could paint his boat, pull in the crab-pots, prepare his sea-trout net and catch up on a little sleep in the sand dunes, gently browning himself under the sun. In fact there was always something fresh and of interest coming along; for his skills as a yachtsman were well known, and he was frequently enticed to crew in one of the many regattas that took place around the coast. Everybody wanted his services at that time because no one else could even approach his knowledge of the currents, the channels and the subtle shifts of wind direction. Shino had a feeling for the shoreline that had been bred in him from his boyhood, probably even genetically through his forefathers, and it showed in everything he did and said.

At that time Shino was in his physical prime, and nothing showed this to better advantage than the greasy-pole competition, held on the last weekend of every August. A great, long telegraph pole was secured across the creek and daubed liberally with grease, and a flag attached to its far end. The rules of the game were quite simple, merely to negotiate the pole, reach the flag, clutch it firmly and swim back to the bank with the prize. Described like this the task might sound easy, but out there, over the gushing tide, it was a different matter altogether and a very intimidating one indeed. Most competitors inched their way along, teetering a little left, a little right before falling in with a great splash and a roar of laughter. A few brave souls would walk out briskly, try to look nonchalant, get halfway or so and then drop off, to swim with powerful, practised strokes back to the shore.

Not so Shino. As holder of the trophy, he chose to perform last, partly so that he knew what he had to beat, but largely for maximum theatrical effect. By then the crowd was wound up and thoroughly excited, and keenly awaiting his usual extravagant annual display. Very rarely would they be let down. The pole would always be re-treated with grease before this last attempt, an operation greeted with great cheers and merriment. Shino encouraged this, for it made his glory even greater, and impressed on every single spectator just how magnificent at the game the mighty poacher was.

This was an occasion for which Shino took the greatest care over

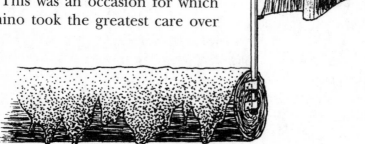

his appearance, virtually the only time in the entire year that he did so. He would stand there in denim shorts with a dark blue smock, which he would take off as his name was called to reveal his great golden chest. Then, unlike all the other competitors before him, he would begin his run fifteen or twenty yards behind the pole, vaulting through the lavender and heather, springing like a savage and leaping onto the pole at hurtling speed. The momentum of his charge would propel him forwards, arms pumping, legs a blur, bare feet racing over the greased wood. Inevitably, invariably, the flag would be in his hand as the crowd let out its collective gasp, and his brown body would flash, triumphantly, into the creek. What the penalties of failure could have been, a slip, a straddle, a nail hit at speed, nobody there dared even think ... except perhaps Jervis, always a gloomy, sour face in the crowd.

This annual fête had other delights as well, notably a race from the village across the mudflats to an old smugglers' watch-house and back again. It was a course that demanded the greatest stamina and the most intimate knowledge of the terrain, and one which attracted a great deal of interest and attention. Once again, if Shino bothered to enter, he invariably won. The only consideration that kept down the number of times he appeared was that he was likely to tackle the race in a different way on each occasion. Once, for example, he took the trophy on horseback because he knew that the tides would be low and the hot sun would have dried out the path sufficiently to allow the creature to canter and then gallop out to sea. The pair made a magnificent sight, and the race was won in record time. Another time Shino took the trophy in a canoe, setting out at low water and coming back with the flowing tide. Once he simply ran there and back and just outpaced the opposition. The only time that he lost was when he swam out on the ebb, hoping to sail back with the wind which ultimately played him false and left him becalmed, a quarter of a mile from victory.

They were marvellous, thrilling times; and not least when a
film crew came to the village to recreate a turn-of-the-century
drama. Shino was paid six pounds a day – a fortune then – to
teach the star the local dialect. Naturally this education took
place in the bar of *The Admiral,* and Shino soon found that the
job was laced with perks. He and the screen-god simply chat-
ted the hours away, talking about life and love and poaching,
and soon became firm, if unlikely friends. Shino's involvement
did not end there, for the star demanded that Shino was given
parts wherever possible throughout the film. So when it was
eventually screened in the local town, everybody trooped
along to see Shino hitting out in the cricket match, proposing
a toast, even singing a verse of a rude song whilst astride a table,
decked out in Edwardian clothing. And there was a final twist
to this tale: filming took place principally on the Bay Meadow
estate, and Jervis himself was employed to help build the set
that Shino could prance on for the ever-rolling cameras; so the
poacher's triumph was complete.

My second summer with Shino saw a particularly dramatic
episode which brought the clash between Shino and Jervis
once again into the sharpest possible focus. In fact, this time,
the entire village was set against the keeper, and for the best
of reasons. Great was the local anger when one June it was discovered without any doubt at all that Horatio, the great and
famous carp of Badger Pit, had been stolen and transported
into the newly dug pool outside Bay Meadow Hall. The village
boys had reported the fish missing first of all; for years they
had trooped over the fields at the first sign of warm weather
to the village pond to watch for Horatio to appear on the surface after his winter slumbers. Moreover, their fathers had
done the same, for Horatio was a very old carp indeed and
his first sighting was always greeted with joy, an indication
that summer was at last on the way. Some people would even
try to forecast how good the forthcoming summer was likely
to be by the date on which the great fish surfaced, Zeppelin-
like, to public view. Thus if Horatio came up on or before

10th May, then the summer would definitely be a happy one; but if his great scaled back appeared after that date, even the farmers took notice and acted accordingly.

No one was quite sure exactly how old Horatio was, but some swore their grandfathers had seen him first, and had even caught him, so that had to be at least fifty years before! Horatio was certainly as big and gnarled and impressive as any oak stump; but then very often the heart ruled the head in the village, and the more informed decided that the great fish had only really been present for twenty years or so. Whatever the truth of the matter, Horatio was held in great affection and loved by all.

The other contention was that no angler had ever landed the big fish, although this was also palpably untrue. Two photographs at least gave testimony to his fallibility, though the locals would still protest. 'That isn't any ordinary mortal fish', Shino would declare. 'I've seen that look in its eye, rolling around as big as a cricket ball in its wise old head. I've tried to catch him, 'course I have, but I've never got nearer than any other man round here. It's my belief that fish will die uncaught.'

It was with horror, therefore, that the lads of the village were proved correct and May gave way to June and even July without any sign of Horatio at all. There was a lot of debate about the matter, and most concluded with the greatest sadness that Horatio had succumbed sometime in the winter; and so the affair began to fade out of local gossip. That was until Pip the postman reported that he had seen the great, scaled talisman of the village swimming around happily in new accommodation just outside the hall. Predictably, there was a loud outcry that the great fish from the village pond, owned by all, had been stolen, transported and placed out of bounds on private property. Who dared do such a thing? Shino voiced village opinion when he put the full onus of blame onto Jervis, the keeper being eager to curry favour with the squire.

Many possible solutions were discussed: a favourite was to go and net the new pond and take everything possible out and leave it denuded, especially as Pip had reported seeing many expensive and glamorous koi carp in the pool. Others urged a more delicate approach, and it was finally decided that all the facts of the case should be discovered. After a full week of investigations a certain Ching eventually came forward and confessed all, one emotional night down at *The Admiral.* Jervis he swore, had put him up to the whole thing, offering him ten pounds to net the village pond and to take the great fish up to the Hall. Ching had been reluctant, but Jervis had a great deal of sway over this rather unsuccessful amateur poacher, and threatened dire consequences if his demands were not carried out. The pub was in turmoil, and it was only Ching's obvious fear and remorse that stopped him being taken out, then and there, and thrown fully clothed into the quay. As it was he was put to better use.

Shino bundled him out of the door, into the van and drove him straight to the doctor's house. It was well known that the doctor tended to be sympathetic to village people and local concerns and was never afraid of speaking up when he felt justice had been ill-served. Though it was nine o'clock at night, he was quite prepared to listen to Shino's tale and Ching's second confession. A phone call was made, and the three of them drove to the Hall in the doctor's car.

They were greeted by the squire, settled down with a whisky each and Ching, for the third time that unpleasant night, told his tale. The doctor then spoke up for the village, explaining that Horatio was an important figurehead, almost something rather sacred, just as the great fish of the Ganges are to the Hindus there. It was Shino who spoke last, and to full, unbridled effect:

'I do know, sir, that you and I have not always seen eye to eye, as it were, but I do think that my own case has often been put to you in a false way. You and I might well disagree about the hares and the pheasants hereabouts, but you are a fair man and there can be no doubt that this fish does not belong to you and must be brought back to its proper home. It was not just taken from one man but from a whole village, and that is simply an evil thing to do. There must be some honour, sir, there must be some respect amongst us that love the countryside as we do, and we are here now to appeal to your sense of fair play, sir, as a gentleman. So, what shall I tell the boys back home?'

As the doctor had guessed, the squire was coolly horrified by this tale, and said that he would put the matter right at once. Jervis would be spoken to (a smile welled up beneath Shino's stone features), Ching would be given ten pounds to net the carp once again and to take him home, and the village boys could rest assured that such a thing would never happen again – they would even be allowed to fish the fine new pond outside the Hall on three specified days each year. 'Right,' Shino proclaimed half an hour later back in *The Admiral,* 'will always triumph over wrong!'

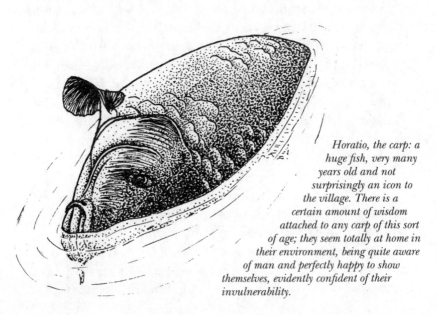

Horatio, the carp: a huge fish, very many years old and not surprisingly an icon to the village. There is a certain amount of wisdom attached to any carp of this sort of age; they seem totally at home in their environment, being quite aware of man and perfectly happy to show themselves, evidently confident of their invulnerability.

11

Billy Burbot

Shino was always quite capable of digressing into complete and utter fantasy, and that was probably his greatest gift as a poacher. You see, no one, least of all Jervis, could then predict with any accuracy what he would be up to next, or how he would solve a certain problem or react in a particular crisis. A great many men will live the same life, following the same pattern, doing the same thing until the day they die, but not Shino. He made it a point of honour that every day should be a little different from the others in his life; only then could it be special and unforgettable. He used to say that this was his philosophy because he had seen his father die a long, slow and painful death, and so had learned from him that life was precious and short; but then at other times he would also say that his father had died at sea – although the moral was pretty much the same, either way!

It came as no surprise, then, that Shino should have found a newspaper report claiming that the burbot was extinct in England, and offering a £1,000 reward for anyone who could prove otherwise. For anyone not knowing a Billy Burbot, he is an eel-like, mottled, bewhiskered, bottom-loving, refuse-feeding, ugly fish, a yard or so long, that tastes just as bad as he looks. Local names in the village for this slimy, quite revolting creature were commonly 'eel-pout', or to those who remembered him well, 'Billy'. '£1,000 for owd Billy! Well, that's a result,' Shino crowed, thumping the paper with his fist. 'The boys round here caught bucketfuls of them when I was just a mite. I remember seeing hundreds in my school days. They were rubbish fish though: nobody would buy them, so I suppose everybody just gave up catching them and wasting their time. But old Billy Burbot will still be there all right, it's just knowing where.'

The extraordinary eel-pout, or burbot. It is sad, in certain ways, that this fish has disappeared from England; the last one was probably caught about a quarter of a century ago, just about at the time Shino was making his abortive efforts. There has been a great deal of discussion as to why these fish have disappeared from England; most people have concentrated on the changing nature of agriculture, suggesting that chemicals infiltrated the waters it inhabited and caused its downfall. A far more probable reason, however, is the succession of warm winters we have had since 1963. Burbot spawn beneath the ice, and need really cold winter temperatures to survive.

It is highly probable that the burbot in fact found England to be very much at the edge of its range, and possibly it has come and gone over the centuries as winter temperatures have dictated. Burbot are still plentiful a few degrees further north in Denmark, in Sweden and northern Germany for example. My own solitary meeting with a burbot was most unexpectedly in Siberia, where temperatures really do plummet. The burbot is not particularly missed in this country for its eating qualities: the liver was always, supposedly, highly prized but certainly my Siberian burbot was a disaster. First of all it was like eating wood-pulp, which then changed to chewing gum, and finally to a most repulsive slimy putty which I, for one, refused to risk swallowing!

So, off Shino and Lucy went, to see old Tip Up down at the cottage on its own behind the church. Tip Up had been the village window-cleaner, a small, wizened, wise-looking creature, but his legs had long ago become very shaky, even though his memory was sharp. 'Oh yes, Shino boy. There were plenty of those owd Billy's around before the war. Bagfuls of them if I remember right.' Shino nodded confidently at this, and Lucy gave a wiggle of delight as the old window-cleaner passed her a piece of cake. 'Oh yes, boy, I remember where they were, too. They used to gather up in that dyke on the east end of the marsh in their thousands in the spring. S'pose they were there for loving or some such. We'd get them easy on worms, we'd dab them, least ways me and your dad would. We be at it all through the summer, taking down a few bottles of beer, sitting on the grass down there just watching the world go by. Good owd days they were. But I tell you Shino, they are horrible owd things and I can't see for the life of me what you'd be doing with one.'

Tip Up leaned forwards on his stick, his eyes bright with curiosity; but Shino didn't intend sharing his £1,000 with anyone and just jumped up, thanked him and said he'd be along with a bit of tobacco and a bottle or two the very first Billy that he caught.

He and Lucy positively sprinted back over the field towards the village; the money was well spent in his mind by the time they reached the cottage again, Lucy's tail a blur at the word 'bones'!

There was no doubt that Shino was as excited as he had been for a long time, but even so, he did recognize one problem. For twenty years or more the whole east end of the marsh had been a nature reserve, and Shino's presence had long been unwelcome there; thus official access to Billy's dyke would never, ever be given. Once more, it came down to a question of visiting during the night.

By then it was early summer and conditions were quite perfect; besides, Shino hadn't been on the east marsh for a while and set out to check it over for a couple of nights. The last of the bird-watchers left the hides there between 9.00 and 10.00 in the evening and the warden, Boomer (after the bittern) was, unfortunately, brother-in-law to Jervis so joined in the general family persecution of the poacher. The good news was that Boomer was even less industrious than Jervis and almost invariably gave his last look out over the marsh a little after the last twitcher had left. By 10.30 to 11.00 p.m. the whole area would almost certainly be quiet. True, the main dyke did stand out very visibly amongst the open marsh, totally exposed to the windows of Boomer's house, but Shino remained confident that he would get in and out and have Billy on the bank before anyone spotted him. Moreover he was blissfully sure one night, perhaps at the outside two, would do the job.

Purist that he was, Shino set out to do the job correctly and catch Billy the time-honoured way, by babbing. He therefore got together first a bucket of worms, and second, an assortment of ragged red wool, a short stout rod and line thick enough to hoist Moby Dick ashore. He waited for a warm night as Tip Up had suggested, one with enough moon to paint things clearly but with some cloud to blur his own outline if Boomer should happen to look out at bed-time. Shino also knew it would be an error to take the van anywhere near, and left it standing in the yard, setting out as the sun began to drop in the west, knowing he had a good hour's walk following the old marsh path created by sailors, smugglers and seamen of generations past.

The track led him steadily east, first on public land and then over fields, past annoyingly curious bullocks until he came to the fence of the reserve itself. He had been quite unseen and now hung, hungry as a fox, looking out over the blackening reed-swamp to the dyke that was bright against the silvery sky. He thought he would just wait a little yet. There was no hurry; he had until dawn, or at least a little before, when the first of the birdwatchers would re-appear.

Besides he remembered, rather soberly, that he had never actually used the old babbing method himself, and so thought he might as well try it out before getting to Billy's home over the fence.

It was just as well he did. If you have not babbed yourself, if you have not had someone to show you how, then trying for the first time, hidden and in the dark, is not to be advised. Obviously, tying the pieces of wool together into a small red parcel was not difficult, nor was attaching this parcel to the line itself, but when it came to baiting the worms onto the wool then every problem imaginable emerged. 'Thread the buggers on, my arse,' hissed Shino through clenched teeth, as worm after worm fell out of the wool to wiggle away into the darkness.

It seemed to him that half the pail had been used up before a reasonable bait was swinging there, against the night sky. He gave it a shake and then, reasonably satisfied, hopped over the fence, skirting the dyke until he found a depression where he could crouch, hidden by reeds, looking over the reserve to the coast road and Boomer's cottage window half a mile away.

It was going to be a miserable night for Shino: the midges were especially bad because of the cloudy, windless weather and the worms just would not stay in the wool more than a minute, no matter how he tried and what methods he used. Each time he eased the bait in, the wool would be empty, except for just once, when an eel the length and thickness of a farmer's bootlace actually swung there, trapped by its teeth that had become entangled in the wool.

By one o'clock in the morning he was utterly maddened. He crept off the marsh and made his way back to the village, to be in bed by 2 a.m., a thousand pounds no better off and cursing his luck. But he never gave up. The bit was firmly between his teeth, and the next three nights saw him with rod, line, worms and proper hook in that same little depression on the dyke. Pots of eels and a flounder or two came his way, and there was even a trout that had entered the dyke somehow from the estuary; but of Billy, not a sign – though in fact that is not quite true. On the third night Shino hooked something far more substantial than any of the eels he had landed so far, a creature that kept on the bottom and wriggled hard, that wriggled so much it got away! The black air was blue. Shino was convinced that Billy had been there, and had gone; and for him it was like throwing fifty pound notes in the air, losing that fish. He went home in a deep sulk, so gloomy that not even Lucy knew how to cheer him up.

Desperation had really set in now; the next day he went out to the shed and hunted around until he came across his old fyke net that he had last used for eels a few years before. He laid this out in the yard and checked it carefully for holes: Billy was not going to get away again. The fyke net was heavy, and he had to carry it all the way in the warm, sultry evening air. And when he got to the dyke his problems continued because of course he had no boat there from which to lay the fyke net, and so he had to strip, slide into the water and lay it by hand. It was an unpleasant task, and Shino could feel the eels wriggle between his toes; but eventually the task was done, and still Boomer was noticeable only by his absence.

Shino slid up into the long grasses on the bank and slept for three or four hours while the fyke net did its worst. He pulled it in before dawn, and emptied out another binful of eels; he simmered quietly, staring with hate towards Boomer's cottage. The light was growing, so there was nothing for it but to lug the wet, slimy, smelly net back over the marsh to the village. A week had passed and still no Billy.

At that time Shino happened to be helping with some sugar-beet hoeing, and would walk staring fixedly at the rows, Billy on his mind. At lunchtime the farmer came down and shared a couple of bottles of beer and a word or two. He had an acquaintance, it seemed, who was out farming some black fen. He was having trouble with old oak stumps buried deep, and the only way to get rid of them was with gelignite. A water-

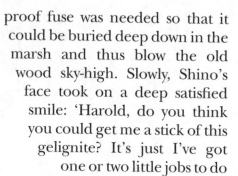

proof fuse was needed so that it could be buried deep down in the marsh and thus blow the old wood sky-high. Slowly, Shino's face took on a deep satisfied smile: 'Harold, do you think you could get me a stick of this gelignite? It's just I've got one or two little jobs to do and I could use something like that more than I could tell you.' Harold was an honest countryman, and said at once that he would see what he could do.

He didn't forget; true to his word, a couple of evenings later he was knocking at Shino's door: 'I've got you a couple of sticks, just like what you asked for, Shino. Take care though, mind. This stuff will blow you and the dog halfway to America if you get things wrong. I'll be damned if I know what you want it for, anyway.' 'Harold, my old friend, if I'm successful because of this then you'll know right enough, and I'll do a day's beet hoeing for nothing and treat you to a night in *The Admiral* afterwards. How does that sound?'

Shino thought long and hard about all this: he knew the power of the stuff lying there on his table, and he carefully cut just half a stick. He stared at the half-stick, and then had second thoughts. After all, he'd have just one shot so surely it was best to take no chances at all. He put aside the half-stick and picked up the second full stick.

Shino slept fitfully, and the alarm clock woke him at 2 a.m. He wanted to get to the dyke just on the point of daylight, for he considered that he would need to be able to see Billy when he surfaced, stunned from the blast. There was light in the sky and the first skylark was singing when Shino lit the fuse. He looked at it for a couple of seconds, prayed, and lobbed the stick into the dyke. Nothing happened for half a minute and then … Billy didn't come up, but everything else did: eels, crabs, weed and most especially the silt of centuries. In an agonised split second Shino saw the grey cloud looming, but he was totally unable to get out of its way. The blast shook Boomer's window and the warden leapt out of bed, knocking over the table, struggling for his binoculars. A strange sight met his eyes: there was the unmistakable tall figure of Shino, slipping, sliding, staggering away to the west. But it was only his height that gave the poacher away, for there were no recognizable features, just a great pillar of mud and weed.

12

Shino's Sea Trout

There is a popular misconception that the sea trout is a fish of the north and west rivers, of flashing waters and lochs blazing in sunlight beneath mountain ranges. True to a certain extent, but in fact large runs of sea trout move down from the Scottish east coast each summer to feed in the shallow, warm waters of England. Here they find sand-eels and peeler crabs, and even small herrings for the bigger fish. Shino knew this, and more than that, he knew exactly where and how these summer visitors could be caught. This was ancient knowledge, passed down from generation to generation, kept within families such as Shino's and guarded jealously; Shino had first gone out with his grandfather almost thirty years before, as a tiny boy, and had noted even then how, when and where to work for the best harvests that the sea could produce.

The first method that Shino used was legal, at least it would have been legal if he had bothered to buy a licence. In the depths of his shed lay a large, cavernous net, far bigger than any of the ones used for birds; and in July, on a still afternoon that heralded a glorious evening, it was pulled out and spread all the way down the courtyard. It was not in perfect condition: mice had nibbled it here and there, and gaps were depressingly large and frequent. Shino, though, was ever the optimist, and told Mears categorically that the net would be ready for the night-time; and so it was, even though the three of us had to work furiously to patch up the holes.

The sea trout is a magnificent creature: it is, in fact, a form of brown trout that has adapted to living and to feeding in the sea, which means that it grows rather larger on the extravagant food supplies there. It also takes on a silvery sheen which makes it not unlike a salmon; in fact, very many people can confuse the two species. The drawing depicts a salmon: note how the mouth only extends to the eye; in the sea trout, the angle of the jaw would push back another half inch or so. Also, a sea trout would probably have more spots on the gill cutters.

The method could not have been more simple: one man held up one end of the net close to the beach, whilst the second coiled the net into the rowing boat, rowed out from the breakers, completed a big loop and then headed back in to the shore. There the boat would be met by the third member of the team who took the net, and between the three of them, the meshes would be pulled in, with whatever was entrapped.

When it comes to catching wild things, simple is often best and this was the approved, tried and tested method that all the Shino family had used since the nineteenth century. And it worked, and worked well.

There were glorious nights that particular summer, generally still and warm with a honeyed lushness to the air. It was fine to sit on the pebbled beach, waiting for the half-darkness to seep in, watching Russian tankers, lights aglow on the horizon and the owls flitting like ghosts on the marshes behind. Talk would be slow, relaxed, of the winter to come, of Jervis, of fish and of village people. It was good to stretch out on the pebbles, watching the afterglow fade and the stars begin to twinkle bright, knowing that the night's work would be exhausting, gripping and productive.

The first haul would take place a little before midnight, and work would continue without pause until four or even five o'clock if there were plenty of fish around. Some nights it was hard to give up, so many sea trout were lying off the

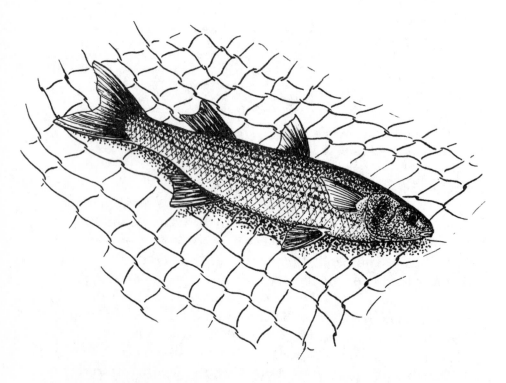

Sea trout were not the only fruits of those summer night netting sessions. Almost as prized were bass, and to a lesser extent grey mullet. Mullet are true wanderers, and spend our winters down in the warmer waters around the Mediterranean and even the southern Atlantic. They begin to return sometime in May or June in vast shoals. They are, however, exceptionally difficult to net because they leap like gazelles; once the leader finds a way through or over the net, the pack is almost bound to follow. Sometimes netsmen may watch, helpless, as a hundred prime fish disappear into the night totally free, a highly frustrating state of affairs.

beach, arrowing through the shallow, still water, shearing through the phosphorescence, hammering into the shoals of sprats and making them fly like raindrops.

Sea trout; even the name of the fish spells magic to me today, a memory of gleaming silver in the shaded night. The smell of salt, the feeling of seaweed on the hands and Shino's merry laughter, forty yards away on the whispering sea. As the first true lights of dawn began to creep in, the chances were that there would be a pile of silver on the shingle, fish between 2 and 8lb, with the occasional monster of 10 or 12lb or more.

'Breeze' would be up, cleaning his shop from 6 a.m., and we would weigh the fish, collect the money and divide the spoils; then it was home to bed, trying to sleep while the mind raced and visions of the fabulous, leaping, silver fish darted again and again through our dreams.

There were, however, ways of catching sea trout that appealed more to a the poacher's instinct and could be even more rewarding financially. As Shino explained:

'You see, there are a lot of fish that will follow the coast right round and get as far as the east mouth, round the point, and there they'll taste the freshwater that comes in from the river. They just can't resist it, some of them, and they'll trace it right up to the river mouth itself. Once they're there, there's no stopping them. They'll push up, through the sluice, through the meadows, into the wood and right up to the deepest pools by the mill. The thing about it up there is that the water is deep and cool, perfect even when the weather's hot. That's where you'll find them, letting clear, cold water through their gills – they love it, and in the evening time they go crazy. But they're quick runners. You've got to be sharp or you'll miss them. It only takes them a day or two to get to the mill, they'll hang there, see there's no way forward and then they'll drop quickly back to sea and start feeding out there again; so you've got to be in and out, quick as the fish. It's all a risky business because you've got to move up there before dark and you can actually be seen from Jervis' cottage through field glasses. It's a cheek, and it's dangerous, but I know Mears is in, and I haven't missed out for over a dozen years, and I'm not going to now. Not with a summer as good as this.'

The good poacher never neglects accurate, immediate advice: this was one of Shino's golden rules, and was one always preached to him by his own teachers. The road-menders, the postmen, farm labourers: Shino would listen to everybody, and give weight to anything that he thought might be of use. So, too, would the village boys that he would have stationed on the river bridge, above the sluices, at the prime times of the summer. Early morning and late evening he always liked to have one or two boys standing there, just for an hour or two at the right stages of the tide, looking down into the bottle-green waters beneath. The sea trout would be quite visible going through, flashing, jumping, chasing sticklebacks and once the boys came up to give Shino the nod, the game would be on.

'Ten o'clock tonight, lads. We'll meet at the bridge. The three of us stand more chance of being seen, but at least if we're chased we can divide and so probably get away more easily. And anyway, we all want to be in on the fun.' It was nearly dark when we met, but the sky still had a great deal of light in it, without a cloud and with a promise of a moon. The key was to stand there, talking, smoking, laughing and watching, and simply bore Jervis out of the game. He would undoubtedly be watching from his cottage a mile away, up the hill amidst the trees, and from where the bridge was quite visible to a man with binoculars.

At last, around midnight, it was quite dark enough to make the first moves, and Shino led the way from the bridge, very quickly into the dark of a ditch. This led half a mile to an aldercarr, which again was gloomy and offered plenty of cover. Where the aldercarr gave way to open fields was the one dangerously exposed stretch, and Shino moved quickly across it, using what cover he could and keeping low: the sea-trout pool – thirty yards long, five yards wide and two yards deep – was reached in record time.

Total, complete stillness: the night was as quiet as a tomb. The pigeons had stayed at roost in the trees opposite, and that was good for two reasons: firstly, our own approach had been so inconspicuous that even those hawk-eyed birds had not been aware of us; and secondly, their continued presence was a sure guarantee that neither Jervis nor Hawker was lying in wait. The coast was certainly clear.

The fishing itself was no great challenge. The bait consisted of two worms on a large hook six inches beneath a couple of weights; these were simply cast into the head of the pool and allowed to trundle down with the current. The line would twitch, tighten, run through the fingers and battle would commence. And this was how the three of us were involved: Shino was always on the rod and played the fish hard, incredibly so; Mears would wade into the shallow water, waiting to pounce on it as soon as it began to thrash close to the bank – he was like a bear, hunched and bearded in the semi-light, his eyes fixed on the river. The first fish was scooped out, unhooked and thrown back to me on the grass. It was my job to kill it and to sack it, and already Shino was playing the second big fish of the night.

'That'll do. We've got five already and we've only been here twenty minutes. A good night's work, so let's clear off while we can.' Shino was right, he always was. The quick, clean, unpredictable kill is what every master poacher aims for every night he might walk out. We took turns at carrying the sack – nearly 40lb of fish in all – and followed Shino, a different route back over the marsh. Rather than heading back towards the bridge, he cut across to a corner of the meadow, half a mile down the road. There stood three cottages, asleep with no light in their windows. He took the sack, went through the wicket gate of the third cottage and entered a coal shed there. It was a finely tuned plan: old Mrs Crowe was a good sort, a woman who had long known and worked with Shino's family. Breeze would pick the fish up from her the next morning and leave the money on her table; Pip the postman would collect this and pop it through Shino's door by nine in the morning, without a single question asked.

They were the finest times that I remember, rolling back along the coast road to the village in the warm, early hours of the morning. We would be content, a little richer, fish scales on our forearms and the old rod slung over one of our shoulders. Sometimes we would stop, up by the church, and watch the dawn creep in over the marshes; at others we would creep down the yard into the cottage and drink and talk and sing until breakfast time.

These were the moments that I felt closest to the poacher, in the quiet, tired times when I believed that I could see the truths of his life that he often tried so hard to conceal. These were the times when he talked of Polly, of a love that was destined to remain in the bud, never to open. Often I told him he was a fool, that she was still and would always be his; but Shino continued genuinely to feel that nothing good could come of a relationship with a digger, a poacher and a netter of sea trout.

I knew differently. Often I met Polly, perhaps on the downs near her parents' farm or on the marsh-head, and I came to fall in love with her myself. I did realize this love was more like the deadly serious crush of a boy just out of his teens. I did know that it was unrealistic and impossible, and more to do with curiosity than passion; but the feelings were still painfully deep, and all the more so because they could never really be expressed.

So my heart would leap in those days when I saw her tall, graceful figure in the distance, the wind lifting her shining hair. We would hold hands as we walked and talked, and then we would sit on the grass or on the sand and sometimes kiss, but never more than that. Polly never encouraged me, always reminding me of the years between us, and that it was Shino she still loved with all her heart. So, although I knew Polly and knew also that we would never be lovers, I cherished those meetings, and locked every minute, every look and scent, each ripple of laughter into my heart forever.

There were occasions when I would tell Shino about these meetings, that Polly loved him unconditionally and that such a love could conquer all; but he would simply smile and say quietly, 'Bingo, you just don't know, you just don't see how it is around here. We had our chance, and now it's over for ever.'

13

A Night on the Net

Shino sat in the darkened corner of *The Admiral* at the table he habitually used when he needed or wanted to talk. It was early October and just cold enough for a fire in the grate, which burned brightly. Work was quite obviously on the poacher's mind, so it was no surprise when he began to talk about it in earnest.

'When I helped my father and his mates it was partridges we were after, often as not. They used to say then that partridges were every bit as good as pheasants – at least as good to eat, and just as easy to sell. The English bird I'm talking about, not the Frenchman, that I never took to myself, nor my dad. If you ask me, it's a crime there aren't any partridges today, certainly not enough worth going after, anyway. It's all down to the bloody farmers, and everyone knows that. It's the chemicals on the crops that kills the insects, the beetles, just about everything the owd partridge likes to live on. Then, don't forget the size of the machinery these modern days. Those great huge tyres grind everything up or flatten everything down, and the nests of any wild birds have to suffer. Season after season, the numbers of wild birds go down; and that's why pheasants do all right, because the eggs are reared unnaturally and not left out there in the field. Ask me, we'll never see the partridge days again, and that's a crime, a criminal shame.

Remember that – it's not my grandad or any of us that has done the partridge in: it's the owners of the land themselves.'

A long silence followed this speech; and when Shino was in this sort of mood, silence was the best policy because he did not take kindly to interruption. The narrative continued:

'Grandad was a poacher above all the rest in those days. I once saw him noose a bird at fifteen feet when he was over sixty years of age. His hand never shook and his eye was as good as it had ever been. [Mears, on Shino's left, cocked an eyebrow and shrugged.]

Noosing, no one knows how to do that now. Grandad had this great long slither of wood – a strip of willow I guess it was – with a horsehair noose

The partridge is a much-loved bird, and is fortunately beginning to make a comeback. It has been discovered, however, that putting down artificially reared partridges is actually detrimental to the survival rate of the wild ones. In fact it is far better to build up and improve the habitat of the wild bird if its numbers are to increase. Viscount Coke at Holkham in Norfolk has been a pioneer in this work, and the numbers of partridge are beginning to show some increase on his estates.

In these dark winter days, Shino was usually eager to get out onto the muds for his duck shooting. This is sport of the most exciting kind, and when the wind is high the birds whistle in like bullets.

at the end of it. He'd go to the wood on a really bright night when the moon was like the day and slide up to the bird and pop the noose over it and it would be another in the hand before you could blink. There was no noise and there was no fluttering from the bird either and that was good because it didn't scare the rest. Grandad always said that he could do a whole wood if it was windy, because then the birds were down low keeping out of the top branches. Still nights weren't good because they were right up top and out of his reach. I've still got his hemp net at home. I bet that goes back at least a hundred years because it wasn't even his in the first place.'

'Hemp?' Mears looked vaguely interested, but was too warmed by the fire and the beer to get properly excited. All that was really on his mind was a vague indecision as to whether to go home to bed, or to get drawn into a lingering conversation and even be press-ganged off into the wood.

'Hemp was what they used to use before nylon,' Shino continued after a while. 'It's a lot better, too, if the ground's not wet. If there's much damp about then the hemp soaks through and weighs like a brick. Dry, though, and it's easier on the hands, and I don't think the birds scare as

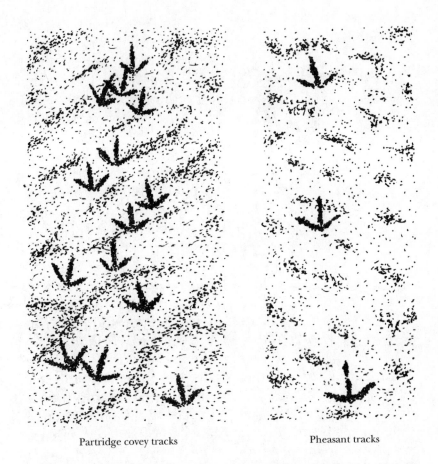

Partridge covey tracks   Pheasant tracks

The poacher will be able to tell instantly, just by looking at the prints in the mud or snow, what birds, whether partridge or pheasant, have been around that day during the dawn or dusk period. Size has a great deal to do with it, but partridges tend to move in coveys or groups and so their marks, as well as being smaller, are generally more clustered together. Notice also how pheasant tracks tend to be roughly in a straight line.

easily, either, as they do under nylon. The hemp's softer somehow, you see.' Again there was quiet for a while, and outside the street looked ghostly white as the moon glinted in through the windows. The weather had been glorious for some days, bright, mellow, a true Indian summer with no hint of a break.

The muds, the marshes and the coastal woodlands have always been the most fertile habitat for all manner of wading birds.

'You know what I'd like to do, Mears? I'd like to give that old net a go. You and me on the ropes, and the boy,' he nodded at me now, 'can string up the birds.' Mears looked non-committal, but Shino was more and more enthusiastic about the idea. 'You know, it's the right time of year, Mears my lad, the trees are still in leaf, and Goose is crying out for birds. There are still a lot of young ones running about and Bingo here [my nickname of those days] can let them go and just string the good ones. I can't think of any reason why we shouldn't have a go.'

Mears shrugged, and then smiled slowly, which was his way of saying the game was on. The meeting was set for three in the morning, three days later at the crossroads pit, half a mile south of a big beet field. Everything was considered with military precision: the moon would be down a bit and the night a little bit darker. The weather forecast continued excellent, and there was virtually no chance of the ground being wet. The field was right on the edge of Jervis' land and so the chance of him appearing so late in the night were virtually nil; Jervis was well known for not liking to get up early. The great thing was that if we were seen around dawn, on our way home, then, of course, it would be easy to pass our appearance off as the start of our normal day on the marshes.

But best of all, the mellow weather had held, had blossomed even, and the pheasants were happy out of the wood, seeing the night out under the stars, in the crops, never bothering to get up a tree all night long. With no hint of frost or rain, the beet field should be full of birds, surrounded as it was by prime woods. A very confident Shino told Goose to be ready for a big bag.

The great hemp net had been dropped off the previous day, all sorted and mended and attached to new, sound ropes. I was the first there by the pit at the crossroads, surrounded by the willows. I had arrived on foot, whilst Mears and Shino were coming on their bicycles, and I hadn't expected to be first. Nor had I wanted to be at all, knowing the history of the crossroads and detesting the atmosphere I felt to be present there: the north shire gallows had stood there years back, the crooked corpses of robbers and murderers swinging under the wide open skies. The land had always been open meadow or heath, and the figures must have been grimly visible to every traveller. Who did not shudder? Who did not brood on their own mortality at the sight of the pain-wracked faces and the vermin-ravaged limbs? Only when the gallows were needed again would the dead be cut down and flung into the pit to rot. That was how the village legend went; and it was on this very spot that I stood in this dark, dead hour of the night.

Operations began at the top end of the field where Shino and Mears laid the net out; in the half light it loomed enormous, far larger than the modern nylon net that had been left behind in Shino's shed. It weighed a good deal too, all those yards and yards of hemp. 'Damn me, Shino, we won't want to be digging this morning after an hour or two of lugging this thing around.' Mears' voice had sounded very loud in the still air. 'Shut up. Git on with it,' Shino hissed, and off down the hedgerow the two men dragged the net, thirty if not forty yards apart, with me following on behind the trailing edge.

We got three birds down the first strip and my job was to kill them and put them on the string. One, however, was a weedy little thing with no tail and I let it go, squawking and running into the hedgerow. When we approached the far end of the field, Shino stayed stock-still whilst Mears took his end in a wide sweeping circle; then they started off up the next strip alongside the way they had come.

The deeper into the field we got, the more birds fouled the net. A few strayed deep in the beet, letting the net go over their heads, but most reared up and fluttered in the hemp mesh long enough for me to get to them and do my deadly business. I didn't care for it a great deal and the old trick of biting a bird's skull with the molar teeth was right out as far as I was concerned. Mears mocked, delighted, but I

Two men working in a field with a drag net. It is a great help if a third is following behind so that he can deal with birds as they are caught up, and the net's progress is not being constantly interrupted. In days gone by gamekeepers would combat the netters by staking out all manner of thorn bushes to impede their progress. Nothing was more irritating in the dark of the night than continually having to disentangle sharp, needle-like thorns from the mesh. Another way was to dig in spiked iron bars here and there; the damage done by these would be more permanent, and could rip the net to shreds. However, the keeper would have to remember where these had been placed, or machinery could be ruined when it came to the harvest period.

had to make do with other ways. Soon my hands were red-
dened, feathers cloaked my jacket sleeves and the weight of
birds on my shoulders grew steadily heavier.

Dawn was a crack in the east when we decided to stop, the
field half done. The net was folded up and taken down the
lane and hidden in a ditch. The birds were hidden in two lots
in holes in the nearby quarry to be picked up later in the day,
after the worm-digging was done; and then it was away to the
muds for all of us for a legal day's work. Mears and Shino
rode their bikes away into the gloom, ready to slide off and
hide in a hedgerow if they should hear a car coming. I cut
my way coastwards through the fields and woods, and kept
such a good eye open for Jervis, Hawker and the rest that I
didn't make a sound, and even came upon a dog fox on his
path home. So, considering the night's work I was well
pleased, and felt I was becoming a promising poacher at last.

14

The Haunted Wood

A wood in the hours of darkness is a thriving place, inhabited by an abundance of wildlife and full of all sorts of noises. The truly professional poacher knows all these, for he is out in the woods at all times, not just on peaceful, calm nights but in storms, in frosts and in driving rain, and he sees the woods in every mood. Woods breathe like an animal or a man, and the poacher hears the sound. Each wood has its own character and the poacher will know it: it can be open, sunny and welcoming or it can be closed, damp with menace. This is not fancy: Shino knew it as a fact.

Shino knew his way round every wood in his own particular world and would travel with as little clamour as a cloud drifting over the face of the moon. He had reached a state of oneness with the woods: they spoke to him, parted for him, yielded all their secrets to him. They certainly yielded their pheasants, and Ladywood was a case in point.

Ladywood was a large spinney with a broad stream running through it, spilling into the lake that bordered its southern extremity. Across from Ladywood lay the park meadows, and then the Hall itself, so any night-time excursion had to be treated as a serious operation. However, a visit was nearly always worth the effort, for Ladywood offered an abundance of roosting sites, in particular a lot of large hawthorn trees which Shino knew were most attractive to roosting birds. Even better, these thorns grew tightly along the stream, and pheasants always prefer to be over water at night; it makes them feel instinctively safer from all types of predator. Moreover at one side of the wood were dense firs, with larches planted in rows between, and pheasants are exceptionally fond of both types of tree as a night-time roost. The bulk of Ladywood, however, was planted in oak, and the pheasants were attracted to these in great numbers, especially in bumper acorn years. Jervis was mightily pleased by these oaks because, of course, they lose their leaves last of all, quite late in the year and a tree in heavy leaf gives plenty of cover to a roosting bird and so makes a difficult shot for poachers. Lady-

Pheasants learn very quickly, even those artificially reared and put out in the wood. If, for example, a cock pheasant can live through its first winter, then it makes a very difficult target indeed in its second season.

Shino often had to deliver birds already plucked and cleaned to private customers, and I was taught one of the quickest ways to accomplish this task. Most people tend to hold the pheasant with the left hand and pluck with the right. However, it is far better to tie the bird from a branch with a string around its feet, and then you can pluck with both hands; this makes for far greater speed. It is also wise to pluck outside to avoid a surfeit of feathers in the kitchen.

How long a bird should be allowed to hang before being prepared is a matter of great debate: Shino liked his own birds, when he bothered to eat them, to be really high and he would often leave them for six or seven days, even in quite mild weather. Most people cannot stomach a taste quite so rich and for them two or three days is about right.

wood really was made for pheasants: to the west, just where the spinney began to thin out, stood the remains of the old wall that once surrounded the nineteenth-century orchard. Occasional birds liked to roost on the crumbling wall itself, but many found a night's rest in the pear or apple trees, especially those trained against the brickwork.

All these things about Ladywood Shino had known since boyhood, but there was something else, something far more extraordinary about the place that he told only occasionally. Just as much as he believed in pheasants, the poacher believed in spirits. This was almost certainly because of his closeness to the land, and his ability to sense its smallest signals. Lucy encouraged him in this belief, and her hackles would frequently, inexplicably rise in certain places in the marshland, in woodland, around churchyards or close to old buildings. Shino would simply look at the changed dog and nod wisely, sure that she sensed what he already knew. Not that these presences ever frightened Shino, for he saw them simply as beings of the countryside like the others that he knew so well. He never bothered to explain what he thought the spirits were, but simply said that they existed in certain places, like mist. However, Shino did know that lots of men were afraid of spirits, and that suited him; it was one reason that he expressed his own beliefs whenever he could. After all, the fewer people there were about the woods at night the better for him, as he well knew; it was not Shino's way to encourage the nervous to wander alone in the dark, and at times he would even do his best to deter the confident.

There was one occasion when a friend of Hawker's, the under-keeper, began to do a great deal of prying along the hedgerows and coverts at night. There was no doubt whatsoever that Jervis was passing him a bit of tobacco money to keep his eyes open and report back what he could. The man, an ordinary agricultural labourer, could be heard a good quarter of a mile away on his bicycle, such a creaking it made, and so really he never got to find anything that would hurt Shino in the least; but a matter of principle was involved. After his evening's investigations were done, the labourer would invariably cycle off home to his cottage down a narrow, steeply sided lane shaded over by two heavy holly trees, quite thick enough to disguise Mears in the first and Shino in the second.

Thus the good man was cycling home one night a little before midnight; the air was deathly still, so tranquil that Mears' low, pitiful moan rang clearly up and down the lane. The bicycle speeded up immediately, cranking faster and faster over the gravel, approaching the second holly bush. As the rider passed underneath, a low but rapidly rising, blood-curdling scream rent the night in two and with a yell to lift his hat, the labourer flung his bike into the ditch and fled for home.

The moon, too, was of interest to Shino in many ways. He had no doubt whatsoever that nocturnal animals and fish were much more active at the full moon; indeed, on those nights he felt the whole world was tingling, on the move, pulsing with energy. And when the moon was biggest he would swear that Shuck was about, a legend that interested him very much. Shuck was a great black dog, a creature with wild yellow eyes and slavering fangs: it haunted the coast, howling at the wind, the devil incarnate. From the cradle Shino had been brought up with stories of Shuck, and had heard so many that its spirit possessed him entirely. Even though seeing the dog is supposed to bring the most hor-rendous ill fortune, the poacher would still look out over the marsh, time and time again, in the hope of witnessing the huge, distracted creature for himself.

Only once was Shino ever actually frightened after dark-ness had fallen, and that occasion was in Ladywood. It was a very still October night and he and Lucy were walking with gun and sack. There was a great number of pheasants at roost, but Shino decided to take them very late because the night was so quiet that a shot would be heard miles off: best, then, to wait until the crack of dawn when Jervis would almost certainly be in his bed.

Man and dog were, therefore, quite content to sit in the long grass by the lake, watching the silvery water under the moon. It was mild enough for carp to be active still, gliding gracefully, leaping occasionally out by the island. Both were enthralled; Lucy was a committed fisher, just as much as the poacher. Some time after midnight, the Hall clock having just chimed, they heard footsteps quite distinctly on the bridge across the stream twenty yards to their right. 'Blast, it's Jervis,' muttered Shino; but it wasn't. The footsteps belonged to nobody, to no visible form, and Lucy's growl bubbled deep in her chest. Even that, however, faded and died as the long grasses along the path that ran towards them began to bend, slowly, as if brushed by a long skirt or cloak.

Right up to man and dog came this eerie presence, and as it passed, it blew ice right into their hearts. Shino felt his whole torso clamped by cold and then a frightening, freezing wind seemed to explode out of him, pushing his rib-cage through his skin as it escaped into the night. The sensation was over as quickly as a hand passing across the forehead, as the grasses beyond them began to twist and bend as the presence departed from them. Lucy whined and licked Shino's hand. He picked up his gun and together they made for home. It was many a night before Lucy ventured again into Ladywood, and Shino made sure that his next visit was in the company of Mears, a man with the imagination of a sugar-beet but the heart of a lion.

15

Dearly Poached

B ay Meadow was one of the few estates in the area then still to contain a herd of deer in its park. This was because the family had been rich enough to maintain its land relatively unscathed since the eighteenth century, managing to weather the vicissitudes of the economic and political climates, notably the agricultural depressions of the 1880s and the 1930s. Certainly during the 1920s the squire's grandfather did have his problems, largely due to his taste for high living, made worse by the slump in farm prices, but the deer park nevertheless struggled on; those workers who survived on the estate just managed to keep the fences up and in decent repair. However, after the Second World War there were several escapees each year and these managed to populate the woods both in and around the estate.

When the squire took over the total running of the farm from his uncle in the early sixties, things began to change: he himself had studied at agricultural college, and he brought a completely new, efficient philosophy to bear on the family's land. Combined with the upturn in agriculture's fortunes, Bay Meadow was soon a thriving concern again. Once the farm and the main house had been fully restored, the squire's attention turned to the deer park where the more decrepit fences were made good, and the pasture attended to. The deer had interbred for many generations and were showing signs of degeneration, so new stock was brought in from Scotland, central England, and even from Scandinavia. That the squire was inordinately proud of his deer park was known all round the neighbourhood: pheasant shooting was one thing, but in the scale of importance, the woods rated far behind the park. To some extent it was the restoration of the deer park that made the squire a national figure in the country magazines; and he relished the work that he carried out, and frequently travelled round Britain offering advice wherever it was needed.

Jervis was not in charge of the deer, and this infuriated him, not least because he knew they were the true apple of his master's eye. The squire had good reasons for excluding Jervis from this park: the keeper was a local man of limited education, brought up with very regimented views, and he simply had neither the learning nor the experience to run herds as important as these: he was overlooked, in favour of a neighbouring landowner's son, a man in his twenties named Troskin. There was an immediate antipathy between the two men: Jervis detested Troskin's educated accent and privileged start in life and, most especially, the air of superiority Troskin immediately assumed. Troskin, for his part, found Jervis sullen and uncooperative, always wanting to dodge any request, failing to hear any demand, and on the few occasions when the squire had been called in to mediate, it was made quite clear that the younger man was the favoured one and that his wishes were to be complied with.

Jervis fumed. His bitterness increased even further when he realised that the squire and Troskin dined together at least once a week, drank copious amounts of the best possible wines and laughed long into the night, by the fire, legs splayed out

A fine study of a red deer with a good set of antlers. There are far more wild red deer in certain wooded areas of England than many people realize, and it is extraordinary how these large creatures can remain undetected. However, they have excellent senses and can move very cautiously indeed when they feel threatened.

amongst the labradors. Jervis' own wife was often called in on those evenings to cook, serve and clear away and she would keep her ear to the door as best she could, trying to pick up any little bits of gossip, any mention of her husband's name. 'Class speaks to class, you know,' she would say to Jervis when he questioned her. 'Slippery as an eel in long grass, that damned boy,' he would invariably snort in reply.

It was widely known that Shino rarely poached deer, and even more infrequently in the deer park itself. If a contact, Goose generally, called for one, then he would sometimes stalk the wild deer of the outlying woods, looking for an animal that was sick, out of condition or simply old. In this way Shino felt that he was doing little harm to the wild population and was simply acting as clean executioner, saving the creature the horrors of a slow decline and probable death in the winter or early spring. Never, under any circumstances, would he take out a fine creature; only if there was absolutely nothing to slaughter in the wild would he venture on the rarest of occasions, within the park itself. This had happened two, or perhaps three times in his entire career – and not, as he was quick to explain, because of any sense of fear or trepidation. He knew that Jervis had little to do with the deer, and Troskin had no horrors for him at all; no, his reluctance was more to do with respect. In a strange, abstract sort of way, Shino rather liked the idea of the deer park, and he also liked the squire a good deal, especially since the affair of Horatio, believing him to be quite a decent man. Finally, if any person showed himself to be a fit guardian of the countryside then he was likely to gain Shino's cooperation, and this had certainly been the case at the deer park.

So, on the very rare occasion that Shino did go in, he did so with the very greatest of care. His aim was generally to kill a weaker deer with a dog, not dear Lucy, because a spaniel is not really up to the job, but with a lurcher borrowed for particular occasions from Sykes, who had the dog trained for just these sorts of nights. Those times that the lurcher was not fit or was not available Shino simply turned the commission down and did not dream of going in alone. For years this had been a point of honour as well as of feasibility.

However, not all those who walk the wrong side of the hedge are so particular. It was October, I was in my second year of apprenticeship with the poacher and the rut had just started up at the deer park. It was always a fine, exciting time, the stags bellowing their challenges to rivals so violently that they could be heard in the village on any still night. It was a blood-curdling, primaeval sound, and when mingled with the hoots of an owl, the bark of a fox and the whispering of the sea on the shingle, it turned the whole place into a magical, fabulous world. On just such a night, late in the month, a large four-wheel-drive pick-up truck appeared near the deer park. There were three men in the cab, seen with guns and flashlights, and on the back was a team of four lurchers. The gang was making no attempt whatsoever to hide itself, quite obviously banking on a silent and speedy blitz on the park. A farm labourer, out for a pint, saw them nearing the deer park; he cycled to a nearby cottage and phoned Troskin at once. Before going out to investigate, Troskin phoned Jervis, demanded help, and then set out to deal with the threat.

Jervis, however, was not in a mood to be rushed. He finished his tea slowly, munching each mouthful, gazing in contemplation at the fire, demanding ever more cups of coffee. He sat in his chair allowing digestion to take its course, only eventually lacing his

The lurcher is a traditional poacher's dog, quite capable of running down a hare or a deer even on its own. Shino certainly appreciated the abilities of lurchers, but did not like them as dogs or companions.

boots in the way of a man dead with weariness. He toyed with the idea of calling Hawker and the under-keeper, and even picked up the phone, but put it down again. 'I don't reckon there's no need for that,' he said gruffly to his wife. He then pondered which gun to take, and which dog, and which route to take to the park; in the end he chose the longest way, stopping to check each snare and trap on the way.

In the meantime, things had not gone well for Troskin: he had come on the men, all three of them, when he was quite alone. They were shooting at deer, either killing or wounding them, and the lurchers then pulled them down in an instant. There were already three dead deer in the pick-up itself, their legs and antlers a grizzly silhouette in the light, autumn sky. At first the poachers were alarmed and were preparing to run, but when they realised that Troskin was alone, they wheeled around upon him and beat him with lead pipes and gun butts, hitting him until he fell; they then took off at high speed, passing Jervis' own vehicle on the lane.

Jervis saw the dead deer, saw the faces white in his headlights and guessed full well what had gone on. It did not worry him in the least; whatever happened in the deer park was not up to him, he reckoned. God damn Troskin and his meddling ways, after all. The lights of Troskin's truck were still burning and the engine still running when Jervis came upon him, lying in a pool of blood. He was breathing and did not seem in such great danger; in fact to Jervis it seemed that the whole episode had worked quite well, and it would do no harm to have the young upstart out of his way for a while.

Troskin pulled through the first dreadful night in hospital, and two days later began to ask questions of the squire: why had Jervis delayed his call for help, and why were the under-keepers not even telephoned? 'At the very least he damn well shirked out, the bastard,' Troskin said, pale under his bandages. 'He let me get it right in the neck all on my own. There was no back-up at all, and he had done nothing to provide it. Nothing. At the worst, I wonder if the man's straight. I didn't mind him stinking like a polecat, but if you ask me, he'd steal your own eyebrows from you if you gave him half a chance.'

Jervis was questioned none too generously by the squire and then by the police, who were keen to trace the poachers' vehicle. But Jervis really had done badly, hadn't even bothered to take the pick-up's number when he had the chance. Sergeant Peggers said finally that he thought the whole affair stank, but unless anything further came to light, he would be obliged to leave it, though with files strictly open. In short, Jervis was under a deep cloud and he was made very aware of this.

Into this potential quicksand, very unwillingly, stepped Shino. Let it be remembered that Sid Goose had done Shino very many favours over the years, buying game and rabbit from him by the trailerful, never asking questions, fencing enquiries and paying in cash, on time and in full. For all his help, Goose called in a favour from time to time and Shino was in no real position to refuse. So in early December when the butcher was asked totally out of the blue for the immediate delivery of a deer by a very valued customer, he knew exactly whom he would contact. Shino knew full well that no suitable wild deer fitted the request, and that the park was the only chance of supply. He resisted, but Goose insisted. 'No. No, Shino, you listen to me for once. This you'll do for me or you needn't bother banging on my door at night with a sack of bloody rabbits. It's a deer I want now, and it's a deer I'll get, and I don't really care how or from whom, but it must come at once.'

The moon was shifting here and there through the banks of cloud that had brought the first scatterings of snow that winter. Shino liked nothing about the night, even though the light was good and he knew that he might be able to get close enough to a deer for a shot. No, it was the absence of any wind that he did not like, and the fact that there was snow about, which reflected light everywhere and unsettled the deer. Nothing was right, not anything about the situation. This was one of the first times in his entire poaching life that he had been forced into a job he did not want to do, not by a very long way indeed. Mears had offered to help, but he was turned down; Shino simply considered that the best chance of complete success was a very quick, very quiet operation, going in and taking the first suitable deer he chanced across, and getting out as fast as possible.

He had walked to the park, keeping to the hedgerows, out of the light, off the lane. His plan was to take a deer, carry it across his shoulders out of the park, through the conifer wood and to hide it in the ruined cottage a quarter of a mile south of the gates of Bay Meadow. He would collect the animal before digging the next morning, drop it off at Goose's, be on the muds as usual and be able to wash his hands of the whole sorry affair.

It was half an hour before midnight. And then Hawker, the under-keeper, was biking home when he happened by pure chance on Shino's footprints leading into the ruin. He made a very wide detour to the back of the building, through the rubble and the old garden and shone his torch in through a paneless window. He looked around and then saw a sack. Hawker knew immediately what that meant, the snow told him its tale. He climbed onto his bike again, joined his original track so it would look as though there had been no pause or diversion, and then made on for home.

At first Jervis did not like being called at ten minutes to midnight, until he heard the reason why. This time he acted with haste, and at ten past the hour, he and Hawker were hidden in the ruin, pressed into the shadows, truncheons in hand. Their breath clouded in the silvery light that flooded the roofless house. Their hearts beat in their temples, their clothes froze in their boots but they never dared even shuffle on the plaster-littered tiles. Their ears strained, desperate for any sound out in the silent night. At a quarter past one came the shot, very faint, quite nearby in the park. 'That's a 2.2! Over towards the farmhouse is my guess. He'll be back in forty minutes or so if he got the beast,' whispered Jervis. 'He'll come round under cover of the tree plantation.'

And so Shino did, his blond hair shimmering in the moon-beams as he flitted from one pool of darkness to another. His sweat mingled with the dead animal's warm blood which trickled down his shirt, matting his chest hair and running down his trousers to his boots. Jervis had underestimated the poacher's strength and his speed across the park: just thirty minutes had elapsed when the two keepers heard the slight-est crumple of snow on the lane outside the ruin.

Shino had paused, as best he could, with the weight of the deer on his shoulders. He crouched down and the blood fell from the animal's mouth and throat onto the snow. Shino did not like the cycle tracks past the ruin one little bit, though he noticed they appeared to be in a straight, unbro-ken line as though the rider had not stopped or pulled in at all. The whole affair stank: the whole night was beginning to scream at him, and his nerves were as tight as bow-strings. All his instincts hammered out a warning to him, but time was racing by and the sack and near-certain safety were hardly five yards off. Still hesitating, Shino made his way off the track and through the old warped door – and fell immedi-ately beneath an avalanche of blows. The carcass of the deer kept much of the worst from his upper body, and without this still warm shield there is every chance that my mentor and friend would have been killed, such was the violence of the blows rained upon him. Even Hawker drew back after the first few seconds, horrified with what he was seeing.

'Stop it, man! Hold off, Jervis! You're mad. You'll kill him, you bloody maniac, you'll kill him!' The younger man finally threw himself on the keeper and the two men rolled in the debris, then drew apart, panting. Shino lay still, blood oozing from his hair. 'We've gone too far this time, a damn sight too far. Take up the deer and be gone,' said Hawker. He knelt and checked the poacher's breathing. Then he laid him over on his side, pulled the sack that was to have been the deer's winding-sheet out of the shadows and laid it over the comatose figure. He caught Jervis up on the road, the older man walking slowly with the weight of the deer over his shoulders. 'This will go up to the Hall first thing tomorrow. Let them tell me I don't know my work,' said Jervis grimly. 'And you, Hawker, you don't know anything about tonight's work, understand? The snow will be gone by tomorrow and there'll be no trace of us having been there. Nothing to link us with that bit of bother. I'll just say that I scared poachers off and that I found the deer in the park abandoned. Just get to your house, boy, get you on home, do you hear me?'

But Jervis was disappointed with his triumph the next morning when the squire gave the dead animal the most cursory of looks. He swore under his breath, and thanked the keeper not at all. 'Tell Peggers what has happened and get rid of the beast as best you can. Try Goose first of all, and tell him to send me the cheque. Troskin doesn't want any dealing in cash, if you understand me,' And that was that: no thanks, no commendations, 'No bloody anything,' Jervis later grumbled to Hawker and then, at nightfall, to his wife.

So Goose got his deer. Towards dawn, Mears had gone looking for his companion. The snow had not quite melted, and the tracks led him straight to the scene of the crime. He got Shino home, but the poacher was sick and he remained indoors until well into the New Year. His ribs were cracked and his hand broken, and there was a scar on his forehead that he would always carry as a mark of Jervis' hatred.

16

Revenge

This was a dark and dangerous period of my poaching life: Christmas came and went, and it gave no joy. Day after long day the wounded poacher simply lay curled up on the settee before the fire, Lucy constantly beside him. Virtually all day, every day, the cottage room was in total darkness, only lit in the late afternoon by the flicker of the dancing flames. Over us all hung an atmosphere of bitterness and pain, whilst Shino began to talk of violence and revenge. The days passed, depression deepened, and all the laughter and joy in life seemed to be at an end.

Neither man nor dog stirred for over a month, and then only to take a brief visit to *The Admiral*, a little way down the street for a quiet talk in the shadows with Mears, Sykes and the rest. His own door was, however, frequently visited, first of all by an exceptionally sorrowful Goose: 'I blame myself Shino, just put too much pressure on you. I knew you didn't want to go and I put my own business first. I know now how it all worked out. I suppose you know that Jervis came to me the next day with the deer that he'd taken from you. Mind you, I don't think it did him a lot of good for I had to send the money by cheque to the squire, and none of it found its way into his pockets, not a bean of it, and the news is that what with all this and what happened to Troskin, Jervis is still pushing his luck up there at the moment.'

Shino didn't need to be told who had jumped him that night in the old ruin; none of us did. The fact that Jervis had sold the deer only served to tell everyone in the village what had happened that night. The weather simply mirrored our mood, desperate mid-winter stuff, weeks of bleak, cold northerlies; the skies seemed grey from dawn to dusk, day after day, with frequent flurries of sleet and stinging wind and frost. There was no snow and there was no sun, and the world shivered.

Mears visited the cottage most days, and he had to take over the lion's share of the digging. He still had orders of three thousand worms or so each tide, and I was only good for around twelve hundred at best. We put in extra hours and worked extra hard and kept the buyers satisfied, but it was scant comfort when Shino barely registered any interest. Moreover, there was more bad news for those like ourselves: one day Mears had to report that the Bear had gone down. The Bear was a giant of a poacher, six and a half feet tall and weighing over twenty stones, who worked the coast further to the west but who had collaborated with Shino from time to time over the years. It seems that he had been caught by a posse of keepers in a wood just after the New Year, and beaten to his knees. It was typical of this man to have fought all the way, and now he and two keepers were lying in a hospital ward. It was as if news of Shino's nemesis had spread through all the estates, giving heart to the keepers, and stirring them to new efforts. In this changed climate, Jervis even began to brag about his so-called heroism, his cunning and his diligence, even though men turned away from him with scorn wherever he went.

Sergeant Peggers visited twice but not a word could he get from the prone poacher. 'Why in God's name protect him,

Shino? I don't see that you've got any reason to lie there silently,' he'd say. 'I'd like you to let the law take due process and not even think of taking matters into your own hands.' Peggers' shadow loomed huge on the wall as he stood over the fire, pleading with Shino, for the policeman had no love for Jervis and a single word would have sent him straight to the squire.

The prone poacher just would not talk. 'I was attacked from behind and I went down without even a struggle,' Shino said, his hands hidden in Lucy's tumble-down ears and his eyes still firmly fixed in the flames of the fire.

'Well, how are you liking all this, boy?' the policeman said, nodding towards me. 'It seems to me like you're beginning to get the idea it's not all a game, this poaching.' He left, and in the silence I looked deep into my mind: the realities of poaching were being revealed, stripped of the veneer of boy-hood larks, evenings of fun in the woodland. What arro-gance had driven me into such a world? Shino, of course, had known the truth about poaching; he had been brought up to it, and preached it by his father and his grandfather, and if there had ever been any romanticism in what he felt about it, this would have been firmly trodden out by their solid, hobnail boots.

Polly was distraught. She insisted that I meet her each afternoon to report on Shino's condition and to deliver gen-eral news from the cottage. 'My place is with him now, I know it is, and I can't stand to be away. You simply must tell him, Bingo, for his good and for my whole life. Tell him tonight, please. I want to move tomorrow, I must. You will tell him, say you will.'

How could I deny Polly any request, deny those blue eyes, that clear face. and not argue her case with a passion and conviction that I felt myself? Shino was too weak to resist me, and the following morning I helped Polly to clear her bedroom up at the farmhouse, and to move her into the heavily beamed back bedroom of Shino's cottage. At once,

the despair that had lain as thick as dust began to lift, polished away by the love and the happiness that Polly brought
with her.

There was the smell of good food from the kitchen, the
sound of laughter and the glow of flowers in the window
where the polished panes sparkled to any light that the dour
days might shed. And as she cleaned or read or wrote, Polly
talked to Shino: now, at last, the man with never a minute to
spare was captive and for the first time had to listen to the
wishes of the girl who had loved him for so long.

Yet, sad to say, storms still lay ahead. Mears was round one
night and he brought with him Sykes, Nick-Nick and Bruno,
Bear's constant companions for over ten years. There was a
seriousness about all the men that Polly sensed, and fearful
of it, she went upstairs. I stoked up the fire, and Mears put
several bottles onto the table and the five poachers sat down
to talk well into the night.

It was decided, after many hours' discussion, that in late
January they would band together and run the Major Wood,
the most prized woodland in all Bay Meadow. It lay, all sixty
acres of it, in the heart of the estate and sheltered most of
the rearing pens. It was a desperate decision, made after the
bottles had been emptied, the fire had worn down and they
had been through all their options. 'If the Bear's not in hospital or in jail then he'll be in with us. I know that, and he
told me to speak for him,' said Bruno. 'Hoppo said he'll be
there, and Ching and Crocky. I've seen them all and they
wouldn't miss it,' added Mears. Nick-Nick said that he would
bring Curly along, a man built like an ox and bald since
puberty. And there was Sykes, whom they all knew would
never move a single night without his long-time companion,
Choppy, another good man to add to the list. This would be
the revenge of all the poachers on Jervis. A statement that
they would not be hounded, that they would not give way.

'It will be like 1901 all over again,' said Shino, now upright
in his chair. 'Then grandad and great-grandad and seven

others took on all the keepers and town police and they won. They didn't lose a man, and they put four of the others out for months.'

There was not much more to be said. Dawn was approaching and the poachers began to make sleeping spaces for themselves around the room, pulling out cushions, re-arranging chairs, building nests like animals of the night. 'And we've even forgotten to count in Bingo,' added Mears, sleepily as an after-thought in the gathering silence. 'Yes,' murmured Shino, 'there's Bingo to add in as well.'

The poachers slept around the fire, and I took Lucy for a walk down to the quayside where the wind bit chunks out of our bones. It was a bleak, cold outlook and I dreaded the thought of digging on the mudflats in only a couple of hours. Even more I dreaded the thought of the coming battle in Major Wood. The intensity of the men that night had frightened me, I make no bones about it, and my heart for everything was being squeezed, wrung out by the cruelty of the winter. Back at Shino's cottage, the air was heavy with snores, and with the smell of clothing none too clean and boots used to fields and woodlands. Mears was growling in his sleep, Nick-Nick was scratching behind his ear; it was rather like wandering into a den of foxes.

The next day, after digging, Polly came out of the shed where I was counting out the worms and packing them up ready for collection. Ostensibly she had brought me a cup of tea but I could tell she wanted to talk. 'Bingo, love, it's time you left us all, you know that. This is all getting too much for anybody who wasn't born to it. People are going to be hurt in the next few weeks, and there's no reason you should be involved. You've been good to Shino and he knows it, and in his heart he wants you to go now.'

Things were no better in my own home. My father, a lawyer, remember, had been contacted frequently by the police, Peggers in particular, over the business. He was aware of what had gone on and what might happen, and he made it quite clear that he wanted to be no part of it, both for his own career and my own good. When I was called into his study, late one afternoon, I knew exactly what I was going to hear. 'Poaching is not your life, and it is not this family's life, in the way that it is to that man. You could say that it is his heritage, and so it is up to him if he wants to continue fulfilling it; but as for you, how can you afford a broken skull or a time in jail? You might have enjoyed this year or so, but it's time for you to move on and to do something with your life and make it your own. I know your mother is happy to have you at home as well, but now I think it's time that you left, for your own good. Put all this sorry episode behind you before it gets any worse.' He gave me no chance to reply, or to justify my relationship with Shino; though I knew justification was quite possible.

It seemed extraordinary that within two or three days a life that I had grown to accept utterly could change so fast; but there I was, sitting by Shino, telling him that the time had come. I remember that he never took his eyes off the fire and merely waved his hand as I got to the door. Only Lucy watched me go, and that, I guess, was because she was hoping for a walk. Long before the end of January, long before the raid on the Major Wood I was in France and I had to wait for nearly a quarter of a century before I heard how the revenge had gone.

17

Shining World

Shino and I left the pub on the evening of our reunion and walked together up the road to the downs that look out over the sea, the village and much of Bay Meadow estate. It was a typical late summer scene, mellow and warm, the stubble fields shining with a golden glow. The pigeons were noisy in the woods of the estate, and the cock pheasants were crying hoarsely from the fields and the hedgerows. We didn't talk a great deal on the walk until Shino plunged into long grasses off the lane; then he pointed out the houses and the farms, the places and people, those who had changed and those who had remained the same since the day I had left so abruptly. A tractor was moving through the fiery dusk to the harbour, its driver a speck of red: 'That's Sykes, ' said Shino, 'working hard still on the land. He gave up digging and poaching a little after you left, and now he's grown all fat and comfortable.'

Shino was still like a hawk, observing and knowing all, giving a running commentary on the world. A moped droned its way down the lane, half a mile off. 'And that, you'll be pleased to know, is Nick-Nick still alive and well. Listen!' There was a long pause between second and third gear of the old machine. 'Still no money for anything, and it will be that way for ever with him. '

I began to say that I was sorry about my departure at a time when I felt I would have been needed; although I had excused it to myself a thousand times in a hundred different ways, it had always remained my own personal stigma. Of course for a quarter of a century, nobody had ever guessed or even known, that I had been a poacher, and the fact that I had been a deserting poacher was a shame that I carried alone.

'You never had anything to feel badly about, Bingo. It was not your struggle like it was ours, and we had no way of knowing how things would turn out in the end. No one said anything against you, not in my hearing. No one. We all realised why you had to go.'

'But what happened then, in the end?' I pressed. And Shino recounted the whole tale:

'It was a strange night and no mistake, and it didn't turn out a bit as we all expected. The plan was simple enough, we were all quite bold and actually wanted to be caught. Seven, perhaps eight of us, I can't remember now, gathered here at the cottage as soon as I was well enough. It was right at the end of the pheasant season and we went as bold as brass by car right up to Major Wood. We'd let it drop here and there what we would be up to, and Jervis and Hawker knew all right and had got themselves prepared. They'd pulled in the keepers wherever they could get them from the other estates – not that many were keen – and they'd even pushed old Boomer into making an appearance! But they couldn't get the police in, no matter how they tried. Peggers wanted nothing of it, and said Jervis was dreaming the whole affair up. He knew all right that something was going on, but he just wanted to turn a blind eye. He owed me a thing or two from the past and he was no friend of Jervis anyway.

So, we got to the wood around eight o'clock and it was right at the end of January and cold. We emptied the first ride. We knew there were keepers about, we just sensed it, you know how we were, and then a whole battery of torches switched on and Jervis steps out, bold as brass. He tells us that we're all under arrest and to leave our weapons there and to leave.

See us, there, Bingo in the darkness. Poachers and keepers, five yards from each other, the steam coming out of our noses. I said to him, 'It'll be you and me, Jervis. This is between the two of us and there's no need to bring in the rest.' But he wasn't having that at all and he called Hawker up and the two of them came towards me. That was when Mears came in. He came down on them like a bull. None of us saw him coming and his whole weight crashed them over. I tell you Bingo, it was just like war out there. Sykes was setting about Boomer and I was after Jervis, chasing him through the trees, burying his ugly old head in the dirt. There were no guns or knives, thank God, not like there might have been in the old days when my grandfather was about, but sticks and fists were going in thick and fast and there was blood a-plenty.

Jervis was squirming and yelling and wriggling under me and a gun went off and a voice called out for peace. We knew at once it was the squire, and we all pulled off. 'That will do,' he said. 'I will not have this brawling on my land. The intruders – and I know who's led them tonight – will go home now, and no questions will be asked by anybody from this estate. My keepers will return to their cottages, and I thank the others for their help. This is the end of the matter entirely and I bid you all goodnight.' I tell you, Bingo, I remember those words today. We all admired the man for his courage and we got up, dusted ourselves down and left at once. We had got in some good punches and felt honour was on our side. You see the whole thing's been burned into me, even though that night was, what, twenty years back, I guess. ['More like twenty-five, actually,' I said.]

Lord, I suppose it is. Anyway, from that night Jervis was on his way out, though we didn't really know it. The trouble for him was that he was of the old school, and the squire was a lot more modern-thinking than his uncle had ever been. Jervis and his like belonged to the past even then, to the old sort of keepering and to the old sort of wood management. Do you remember Troskin? He became general warden of all the estate, a year or two after you left and Jervis was soon on his way. It took the estate a long while to get him out of his cottage, but then he was caught poaching his own pheasants. I was actually called in to give evidence against him, would you believe it – it was up to me to say, honestly, that I'd seen him out at night with Hawker taking birds for themselves. The squire threatened them with prosecution. There was lots of cursing and swearing, I can tell you, but then the two of them packed and they left. Jervis is still in the county, I believe. For years he has had a small shoot in the west somewhere, but I don't see him now, nor Hawker. I haven't seen either of them since the day they packed their bags and left the village. The bad old days are well done with, if you ask me.'

He was reflective for just a short time, looking intently at a hare making its way between some bales of hay in front of the small spinney to the east. 'The estate's run quite differently these days. There's public fishing now on the lake and a wild-flower centre has opened. There are even horse-riding trails. The deer herd has been built up and up, and the whole place is now run along environmental lines. Green! We're as green as lettuce leaves today!'

'And you, Shino? Have you changed that much?'

'I take photographs now, Bingo, not the birds themselves. I've even had an exhibition or two, and you can see the sort of thing I do in quite a lot of the country magazines. The extraordinary thing is that the old poaching skills stand me in good stead in what I'm doing today. If you know how to get up to a creature to shoot it, taking a photograph isn't that big a problem. The two good things are that a photograph pays better, and it's legal!'

'So you don't poach at all these days, Shino?' I asked.

'How could I? I'm even a part-time warden up at Bay Meadow so I don't think the sight of me with my old 4.10 would go down at all well!'

'How on earth does Goose manage without you?' I joked.

'He's retired now, to a little cottage along the coast, and Breeze has gone, too. The village can't provide a good enough living for a fish merchant these days.'

'And Mears?'

'Ah, now, Mears has done well. He went off to art school a year or so after you left, and he's a big success. Wildlife paint-ings for schools everywhere, and his own cottage now on the coast. He's still got the beard and that twinkle in his eye – you know what I mean, I guess – but he's bigger and broader than ever now.'

'Peggers?'

'Retired, too, and so fat now he'd never catch a cold. He still lives in the village and we'll have a pint together in *The Admiral* whenever we meet up. And that's another turn round from the old days, I suppose.'

I chuckled, and we continued to look around the scene that I had loved so deeply so long ago. It was with relief that I realized that nothing had changed greatly to destroy this beloved, precious landscape. Nibbles perhaps, here and there had taken place, but the occasional bungalow did nothing to destroy the overpowering impression of vast, flint-walled churches, proud merchant houses and rows of seamen's cottages set in such lush countryside. Isolation had served this place well, had saved it from the general bland encroachment of development. Isolation and the squire: so privilege could have its advantages, and this was a thought I would have choked on a quarter of a century before, and frequently did those few times my father tried to preach his own gospel.

Through the evening light, up the lane towards us walked a woman with a dog. Her height, the colour of her hair and the easy, graceful stride made my heart leap. So did the familiar bundle of brown and white by her side. Shino saw them too and said simply, as if I didn't know, 'That's Polly and Lucy.'

'Lucy!' I cried, totally startled now.

'Oh, not the one you knew! This is the grand-daughter. When it came to a name for her I felt it was only right to go back to a bitch that had served me so well for more than twelve years. She was a good dog; you knew that. She helped me through some bad times in those days. A truer dog I don't think anyone has ever possessed than the old Lucy.'

'And Polly?'.

Shino shrugged, smiled and merely said, 'Well, why not? I suppose we've all changed a good bit since those days.'

It was good to hug Polly again, feel her arms around me like they used to be, strong, warm and brown, smelling of salt, sand and earth. 'What on earth are you doing back here?' she asked, her old shining smile lighting my heart as it always had done. 'You've been a stranger too long, you'll stay with us tonight. I absolutely demand it!'

'I can see that you're happy then, the two of you. You obviously got him to see the light!' I said.

'I did in the end, but I'll tell you now it wasn't easy. I honestly think that he wanted to die old and alone like some mangy cock pheasant on a tree branch.'

We walked together laughing, the dog racing around us, a blur of brown and white: we reached the village, where the street danced with the colours of the afterglow, and turned into the courtyard that I remembered so well. I felt as though I was returning home at long last as the door swung open and I entered the familiar room. It was as I remembered it: the stuffed badger, the foxes' masks, the antlers on the wall; only now they were dusted, and the spiders no longer ran through them as plentiful as crabs on the quayside. I glanced in the kitchen and looked again. There were two sea trout and a hare on the floor.

'Shino!' I exclaimed.

He just winked in reply, and pulled the door closed on our mutual past.

And so it seems that Shino and his snares will go on for ever...!